W9-CAM-427

Praise for
Completely His

"Engaging and soulful."
—Publisher's Weekly

"Shannon Ethridge's life exhibits God's transforming power. Her response to tragedy will guide others who struggle through dark valleys, to find the light of hope that is in Christ."
—Max Lucado, best-selling author

"When the worst has happened, only time can bring perspective and turn trauma into triumph. Shannon Ethridge is an incredible woman who has a story to tell and a passion to share. Through experiences that would level most, she has risen as a lover of Jesus who can speak to the heart of every woman. *Completely His* calls even the most timid or scarred to a place of deep, sweet relationship with the One who patiently waits for His beloved to lean in and trust Him. I loved the book. I love Shannon's heart."
—Jan Silvious, author of *Foolproofing Your Life* and *Big Girls Don't Whine*

"Insightful and daring, *Completely His* so challenged me to look at myself honestly and ask 'Am I *all* yours, God?' Shannon is completely vulnerable as she shares a longing for God in every area of her life and a step-by-step example of how to walk with Him in all aspects of daily living. This message is encouraging, life changing, and much needed by every one of us."
—Shaunti Feldhahn, best-selling author of *For Women Only* and *For Men Only*

COMPLETELY
His

Other books by Shannon Ethridge

Completely Loved
Completely Forgiven
Every Woman's Battle
Every Woman's Battle Workbook
Every Young Woman's Battle
Every Young Woman's Battle Workbook
Every Single Woman's Battle
Every Woman, Every Day
Every Woman's Battle Promise Book
Preparing Your Daughter for Every Woman's Battle
Every Woman's Marriage
Every Woman's Marriage Workbook
Words of Wisdom for Women at the Well
Words of Wisdom for Well Women

COMPLETELY *His*

Loving Jesus Without Limits

SHANNON ETHRIDGE

Best-selling author of the Every Woman's Battle series

WATERBROOK
PRESS

COMPLETELY HIS
PUBLISHED BY WATERBROOK PRESS
12265 Oracle Boulevard, Suite 200
Colorado Springs, Colorado 80921
A division of Random House Inc.

ISBN 978-1-4000-7110-4

Library of Congress Cataloging-in-Publication Data
Ethridge, Shannon.
   Completely His : loving Jesus without limits / Shannon Ethridge. — 1st ed.
     p. cm.
Includes bibliographical references.
   ISBN 978-1-4000-7110-4
   1. Christian women—Religious life. 2. Ethridge, Shannon. I. Title.
   BV4527.E84 2007
   248.8'43—dc22

                         2007001300

Printed in the United States of America
2007—First Edition

10 9 8 7 6 5 4 3 2 1

In memory of Marjorie Jarstfer

*The passion of love bursting into flame is more
powerful than death, stronger than the grave.*

SONG OF SOLOMON 8:6 (CEV)

CONTENTS

ACKNOWLEDGMENTS

Karen Schulze—I'm not sure I would have ever caught the vision for this project had it not been for our special friendship. You've not only encouraged me to cultivate a bridal love for Christ, but you've also given me an appreciation for my Jewish roots. For that, this Gentile is ever so grateful.

Danielle Kosanovich—many thanks for the multitude of hours you invested in the seminary libraries doing research for this project. You were a Godsend!

Shirlee State, Lyn Souter, Shelly Lewis, and the Shannon Ethridge Ministries prayer team—I couldn't do what I do without your assistance. Thank you for sharing my passion, for your countless hours of e-mail ministry, and for your heartfelt prayers for women worldwide.

Pastor Bob Smith, how we appreciate your strong leadership, encouragement, and friendship. We can't thank you enough for the many hours you invested in the theological review of the devotionals in this series to make sure the interpretations were bull's-eye true to what the biblical author intended.

Ron and Katie Luce, Dave and Beth Hasz, and the female interns of Teen Mania Ministries—teaching the Women at the Well class on your campus is one of my greatest privileges in life, and I am eternally grateful for the opportunity.

Don Pape—thank you for fanning this bride-of-Christ spark into a flame. Your enthusiasm for this series gave me great confidence as this vision was being birthed.

Liz Heaney—how I value your amazing editorial knack, girlfriend! Nobody does it better.

Jeanette Thomason and the WaterBrook team—thank you for your creativity and commitment to excellence.

To all of the women that I had the privilege of interviewing for this book—thank you for generously sharing your time and testimonies. Your lives are an inspiration.

To my family and live-in cheerleaders, Greg, Erin, and Matthew—I am so blessed by your unconditional love and encouragement. Thank you for believing in me.

And to Jesus Christ, my heavenly Bridegroom—let me just say once again, "I do!"

My "Burning Bush" Experience

M y junior year of high school was off to a great start. By the third day, I had finally memorized my class schedule, my locker combination, and most of my pep-squad routines. I can still remember getting ready the morning of August 29, 1984, slipping on my new jeans and jelly sandals, grabbing my books and pompoms, and kissing my mom good-bye.

It was a ten-mile drive to school from our house in the country. As I got into my little brown Plymouth Champ, I grabbed my seat belt, realizing, *I never remember to wear this thing, but I may as well put it on now that I'm thinking about it.* I drove down our oil-topped road and onto the highway that would take me to the interstate. However, I never made it to the interstate that particular morning.

As I came over a hill, I remembered that I still needed to put lipstick on. I adjusted my rearview mirror for a quick application. As my eyes returned to the road, I caught a glimpse of something moving, then felt my car jolt suddenly. In a split second it occurred to me that I had hit something. My initial thought was perhaps it was a cow or other farm animal out of its pasture, but I had a sinking feeling that it was something much worse.

As I unlatched my seat belt, flung open the car door, and ran back several yards to see what I had hit, my sinking feeling was confirmed. I stood trembling in shock over the body of a curly-headed woman lying face down in the grass next to a mangled bicycle. I wanted to turn her over to see if I could help her, but I knew I couldn't waste precious time in calling for an ambulance.

There were only two houses in sight, so I ran to the closer one as fast as my jellies would take me. Pounding on the door, I pleaded for someone to open it. When there was no response, I ran to my car and drove back the other direction, passing the scene of the accident en route to the other house. I was relieved when an elderly man opened the door and quickly moved aside to allow me use of the phone. I called 911 for an ambulance, then called home and asked my mom to drive down the road until she saw me. I couldn't bring myself to tell her anything else.

By the time I got back to the scene, another car had stopped, and a gentleman was standing on the side of the road, near the woman. He looked at my car and asked, "Did you hit her?" I responded through my tears of panic, "Yes sir, but it wasn't a hit-and-run. I only left to go call an ambulance." My mother arrived within a couple of minutes, and I tried to pull myself together as she ran toward me with her own tears of panic. As we waited for help to arrive, all I could think about was that the woman I had just hit was probably someone's mother...someone's daughter...someone's wife. How would I ever face her family after what I had done?

WAITING IN VAIN

It took forty-five minutes for the ambulance to arrive. When a paramedic finally examined the woman, he coldly explained that we would have to call a funeral home because there was nothing he could do. He said it appeared as if she'd been killed on impact, which made me feel as if the past forty-five minutes of hoping and praying had been in vain. Minutes later, the justice of the peace arrived and pronounced the woman dead.

I left the scene not even knowing who she was. The next two hours were a blur. I remember collapsing on the living-room sofa, sobbing, then waking up later when a policeman knocked on the door, asking to question me. I kept thinking, *This wreck was all my fault. I should have been the one killed, not her.* Terrified of facing the woman's family, I considered suicide more than once that afternoon. But my parents had already suffered the loss of one daughter when my eight-year-old sister died suddenly of an aneurysm in 1972, so I couldn't bring myself to cause them even more pain.

After the officer left, I went outside and reviewed the damage to my car. I realized I must have hit the back of the bicycle with the passenger's-side bumper, throwing the bike (and the rider's body) into the windshield and roofline of the car. In fact, the impact had forced the roof on the passenger's side all the way down, causing it to touch the floorboard of the back seat. If anyone had been riding with me, he or she would have been split in half. I thanked God that none of my friends had tried to hitch a ride to school with me that morning.

However, I noticed that it seemed as if an invisible shield had protected the driver's seat. I reached for my pompoms in the backseat, behind the driver's side. As I picked them up, shards of glass flew everywhere, yet I had not received even a single scratch. I remembered how something (or Someone) had prompted me to put on my seat belt that morning, which was an unusual act for me at the time. I now sensed that God must have placed a hedge of protection around me. Wondering if He perhaps had spared me for a reason, I vowed not to commit suicide, regardless of how painful facing the woman's family might prove to be.

A Shocking Wake-Up Call

Later, when my mother told me I had a phone call, the man on the other end said he was calling to inform me that the woman's name was Marjorie

Jarstfer and that he was her neighbor. I didn't know either family, although both lived just a couple of miles from our house. The caller also informed me that he and his pastor had driven to McKinney, Texas, to tell Gary Jarstfer that his wife had been killed in a car accident. My heart sank. The family now knew. I was sure they probably wanted me dead too.

The caller continued, "Shannon, I want you to know that Gary's immediate response was, 'How is the girl? Was she hurt? Does she know it's not her fault?'" I couldn't believe that this man's first response to such devastating news was concern for me, the one responsible for his pain. How could he even think of me, when I had just taken his wife from him?

I was even more stunned when the caller said Gary wanted me to come to his home the night before the funeral, an invitation I wanted to decline but knew I couldn't. The next night when I went to see him, I got out of the car with my heart racing and more lumps in my throat than I could count. As I walked toward the house, I felt as if I were walking in to face a firing squad.

As I entered the house, I looked down the entry corridor to see a big, burly middle-aged man coming toward me, not with animosity in his eyes, but with his arms open wide. Gary Jarstfer scooped me up in the warmest embrace, and the tears that I had been fighting back were now flowing freely onto his flannel shirt, with his own tears flowing onto the top of my head. I couldn't stop repeating, "I am so sorry. I am so sorry." Once we regained our composure, Gary introduced me to his pastor and two of his adult children. Then he took me by the hand over to a window seat and proceeded to tell me things he wanted me to know about Marjorie's life.

"My wife was such a godly woman, and we've served many years with Wycliffe Bible Translators. There was no limit to how much Marjorie loved the Lord," Gary explained. "She had a very close, intimate walk with God, so much so that she's actually been telling me for a while that she sensed the Lord would be calling her home soon. She lived every day as if it would be her last on earth, and she never left this house on her morning bike ride that she didn't hug and kiss me as if she might be saying good-bye for the last time. She was so convinced she'd be leaving this world soon that she just recently took out additional life insurance. Just days ago she even played the flute and gave her personal testimony at our church about how she was ready to leave this world anytime and go to be with God for all eternity."

Gary had my full attention as I tried to wrap my brain around the idea that someone could be so close to God that she would know when her time on earth was about to be up. But what followed astounded me even further, as Gary continued, "Shannon, God was ready to take Marjorie home. Even though this has caught us all by surprise, it comes as no surprise to Him. You may be wondering why God allowed this to happen to you, but I want you to look at it this way. He knew you would be strong enough to handle this, and that's what I want you to do. You can't let this ruin your life, Shannon. God wants to strengthen you through this. He wants to use you. As a matter of fact, *I am passing Marjorie's legacy of being a godly woman on to you.* I want you to love Jesus without limits, just like Marjorie did. I want you to let Him use you for His glory, Shannon."

These weren't just empty words Gary was using to ease my pain. He lived his life just as Marjorie did, trusting in God's sovereignty and submitting to whatever the Lord had in store for his life, regardless of what it might cost him. How do I know? Because of his actions in the weeks, months, and years that followed.

Shortly after the accident, we learned that there had been some confusion about which ambulance service should have come. The wreck occurred just outside of the Greenville city limits, and a policy had recently gone into effect that Greenville ambulances would no longer service calls outside of the city limits. The forty-five-minute wait could have been reduced to only a few minutes if we had not had to wait for an ambulance from a neighboring city. A newscaster approached Gary and asked if he was going to sue the city because it had taken so long for an ambulance to respond. Gary replied, "Of course not. Marjorie died instantly. There is no reason for any kind of action."

A few weeks later, Gary was told that he could likely sue my parents for more money than our insurance policy would cover, and yet again he refused, saying, "What would be the purpose of adding to that family's grief by making their lives more miserable?" The district attorney wanted to try me for involuntary manslaughter, but months later when it was time for the case to be tried in the Hunt County Court, Gary insisted they dismiss the charges without a trial. He had a perfect opportunity to seek justice, yet he chose to extend mercy instead.

> *The notion of God's love coming to us free of charge, no strings attached, seems to go against every instinct in humanity. The Buddhist eight-fold path, the Hindu doctrine of karma, the Jewish covenant, the Muslim code of law—each of these offers a way to earn approval. Only Christianity dares to make God's love unconditional.*
>
> —PHILIP YANCEY, *What's So Amazing About Grace?*

I kept waiting for Gary to come to his senses, change his mind, and finally dish out the punishment I deserved. However, time proved me wrong. For weeks after the wreck, Gary continued checking in on me occasionally, calling or dropping by where I worked just to see how I was doing. His periodic newsletters and annual Christmas cards have been a staple in my life for the past twenty-plus years. When my husband, Greg, and I were entering the mission field ourselves, Gary and his second wife, Betty Ann, came hundreds of miles to our home to pray with us and encourage us.

Gary's merciful actions, along with his challenging words to me that night before Marjorie's funeral, would be my source of strength and comfort for years to come. God took this horrific event and turned it into something beautiful. As a result I can say along with the apostle Paul, "We also rejoice in our sufferings, because we know that suffering produces perseverance; perseverance, character; and character, hope" (Romans 5:3–4, NIV), and "In all things God works for the good of those who love him, who have been called according to his purpose" (Romans 8:28, NIV).

I gradually went from feeling "to blame" to feeling "chosen," chosen to carry the mantle of being a godly woman who loves Jesus beyond measure. I *wanted* to be completely His, not just with my lips, but with my life. However, like most Christians, I've had to learn to love like that. It wasn't something that came naturally or even supernaturally overnight. It's been a long process that continues to this day, a process I'd like to walk you through in the coming chapters of this book.

MY FIRST REAL GLIMPSE OF GOD

Even though I grew up attending church and singing "Jesus loves me, this I know…," I don't think I ever really knew Jesus personally, understood the depth of His mercy and compassion, or fully experienced His love until I met Gary Jarstfer. His response toward me, the one who had caused him indescribable pain and loss, has served as a vivid reminder of how Jesus Christ endured all that pain on the cross, yet His first concern is always for us, those who nailed Him there.

While I'll never be glad the accident happened or that Marjorie was killed, God used it to get my attention in a big way, just as He used a burning bush to get Moses's attention. In the third chapter of Exodus, God appeared to Moses in a burning bush and informed him that he was His chosen instrument to deliver the Israelites out of Egyptian slavery and usher them into a new land. But Moses had a skeleton in his closet, literally. He had killed an Egyptian and buried him in the sand years before. Most likely he didn't want to go back to the place where he had killed someone for fear of what kind of music he may have had to face.

Like Moses, I had been responsible for the death of another, and I, too, believed I was automatically disqualified from ever doing anything great for God as a result. After all, can God really use a murderer to do His will? You bet He can. He chose to use Moses, He chose to use Paul (who intentionally executed Christians prior to his radical conversion), and I somehow knew that God was choosing to use me as well—although for what, I was still unsure.

In the coming years as I recognized that God was calling me into youth ministry to speak to teenagers about saving sex until marriage, I was tempted to "pull a Moses." I questioned the sanity of God's selection, just as Moses questioned God's sanity numerous times in one conversation. "Who am I that I should go?" "What if they ask who sent me?" "What if they don't believe me?" "But I'm not an eloquent speaker!" "Please send someone else!" (based on Exodus 3:11–4:13) Like Moses, I found myself telling God, "Surely You don't realize who You are asking! If You did, You'd send someone else!"

But God used the story of Moses to teach me several things. First, *He doesn't call the equipped, He equips the called.* It was okay that I didn't feel capable, as long as I knew He was capable of giving me what I needed to be obedient. Second, *our fears do not change God's plans, but understanding God's plans can change our fears.* My insecurities gradually disappeared, as I understood my ordained part in God's bigger plan. Third, *accomplishing great things for God doesn't require great talent, only great faith in*

Him. As I have trusted God to equip me, to show me His plans, and to replace my fears with faith, I've discovered there's no greater, more euphoric feeling than knowing that the God of the universe is working in you, through you, and even in spite of you when necessary.

The car accident was my "burning bush" experience with God, and in the years that followed He revealed His desires for my life—desires I'm not sure I would have recognized had He not gotten my attention so fully. He used that season to show me a side of Himself that I needed to see in order to more fully understand His immeasurable love, which is my source of strength and confidence as I continue to embrace this calling I've received from Him.

As my relationship with God has deepened and grown more intimate over the past two decades since the accident, I've come to realize I'll never be satisfied with the kind of Christianity that far too many people settle for. I don't want to be an "I'll do the minimum to get into heaven" kind of Christian. I don't want to be a half-baked, half-hearted follower who submits to the Lord only when it's easy or when there's something in it for me. I want to love Jesus without limits. I want to be a woman who sees herself as the beloved bride of Christ, His chosen helpmate who joyfully pursues His presence and seeks to carry out His will with dogged determination, regardless of what it may cost me personally. I don't want to stop short of any goal God may have for me. When my body is buried in the ground, I want all the angels to say, "She shouldered her burdens with great strength, maximized her opportunities to bring glory to God, and squeezed every blessing out of life that her Creator intended her to have."

What About You?

While you may not have experienced such a traumatic event in your life, have you had your own unique glimpse of God's character? Times when

God's presence or calling was undeniable? If so, I pray you will allow the Lord to stir the already-glowing embers in your heart and set your soul ablaze with His love as you continue reading. If not, I pray you will get your own magnificent glimpse of God through this book and the four devotional books that are part of this Loving Jesus Without Limits series.

The lead book, which you are reading right now, consists of many personal experiences and reflections of my own journey toward loving Jesus without limits, personal testimonies from other women, inspirational scriptures, and spiritual principles you can apply to your own life. Each of the subsequent four devotional books will explore specific characters or passages of Scripture that can help you grasp more fully who God is and how you can appropriately respond to His limitless love for you.

As you read this series, I hope you become convinced that:

You are not just anybody. You are God's chosen. You are His beloved bride.

If you're like me, you may have some questions about these concepts. You may think the idea of being the bride of Christ sounds strange, or you may wonder what it even means. After all, how can we be helpmates to the Creator and Sustainer of the universe? How do we live out this role? My prayer is that by the time you finish this book, many of your questions will be answered.

But for now, rest assured that God understands your hesitancy, and He wants you to allow Him to prove Himself as the magnificent lover, protector, and provider He truly is. Allow yourself to be courted by the Creator, so you can grasp these truths and come to understand His rock-solid, unchangeable, unwavering love for each and every one of us.

While there is certainly no traceable road map toward a more intimate relationship with Jesus Christ, I believe it begins with catching your own glimpse of who God really is—not just what He expects or wants from you, but a glimpse of His very nature. He wants you, dear sister, to know you can never exhaust His mercies. He wants you to recognize His deep longing to be in relationship with you. He desires for you to feel His unconditional, indescribably lavish love flowing through every fiber of your being and out toward everyone around you. He wants you to see Him as your heavenly Bridegroom and to see yourself as His spiritual bride.

Are you ready to be swept off your feet? To be courted by your Creator? To allow yourself to love Jesus as you have never loved anyone before? If so, keep reading. In the next chapter, we'll explore how you can get your own glimpses into the very nature of God.

Glimpses of a Loving God

I walked downstairs to my office and laundry room one afternoon, noticing that someone had left the dryer door open with a load of towels still unfolded inside. Since I lean toward perfectionism, I couldn't just sit down and concentrate on the work I needed to do, knowing that a load of towels was sitting there. I slammed the dryer door shut, turned the knob to "high heat" for thirty minutes, and sat down to pay some bills.

Within seconds, I heard a thud coming from inside the dryer, then another thud, and so it continued in rhythm. I thought, *Hmm... Greg or the kids must have tossed wet sneakers in to dry.* Thinking nothing of it, I pressed on until the buzzer went off half an hour later. Not wanting the towels to wrinkle, I opened the dryer door immediately, reached in, and pulled out not a sneaker, but Miss E, our family cat, dazed and delirious from having used up at least eight of her nine lives during that thirty-minute dryer ride. It took Miss E several hours to regain her composure. She eventually had to have her tail amputated because of the nerves that were damaged. Fortunately, she survived the ordeal, and the children forgave me for being so careless.

Things aren't always what they seem. I had assumed that whatever was rumbling around in that dryer was probably just some worthless old sneakers, but it turned out to be something precious to every member of our family. Had I not reached inside to fold those towels immediately, Miss E surely would have died from heat exhaustion. In order for her to survive, I had to reach in and grab hold of her.

God's nature isn't always what it seems either. Before the car accident, I saw God as a heavenly kill-joy...an angry disciplinarian...a disinterested, distant being who was exasperated by my failed attempts at getting my spiritual act together. Had I known that God's nature is so merciful, so gracious, so patient, kind, and loving, I would have embraced a close relationship with Him much sooner than I did. I'm just thankful that God, in His goodness, has since given me such intimate and personal revelations about His true character.

Get a glimpse of God's true nature, girlfriend. He can't do wrong by you. Regardless of who or how many have left you, neglected you, or hurt you, you'll never have to count God as one of those people. It's not just that He won't. He can't. His very nature makes it impossible. So rest assured: you can't wear out your welcome. You can't do anything good enough to make Him love you any more than He already does, nor can you do anything bad enough to make Him love you any less. God is unchangeable, forever committed to His love relationship with you. Only He is capable of loving you without any limits whatsoever, and only He is deserving of your limitless love in return.

Of course, I'm not the only one who has ever found this hard to believe. Rather than recognizing God as such an extravagant lover, many people see Him as a harsh, impossible-to-please, judgmental disciplinarian. I have a Jewish friend who, when I mentioned how fascinated I was with Jewish history and how the Jews are God's chosen people, retorted, "Chosen? For what? Misery?"

Have the Jewish people suffered misery? Anyone who has read the Old Testament or walked through a Holocaust museum wouldn't be foolish enough to try to deny this fact. But was God unfamiliar with their plight? Absolutely not. If anything, God is the only one who kept them from extinction, by their own deeds and by the evil deeds of others.

Indeed, no one's plight in life goes unnoticed by God. He alone is sympathetic to every suffering known to humanity. Consider the following piece of prose that vividly illustrates this truth:

At the end of time, billions of people were scattered on a great plain before God's throne. Some of the groups near the front talked heatedly, not cringing with shame but with belligerence.

"How can God judge us? How can He know about suffering?" snapped a joking brunette. She jerked back a sleeve to reveal a tattooed number from a Nazi concentration camp. "We endured terror, beatings, torture, death."

In another group, a black man lowered his collar. "What about this?" he demanded, showing an ugly rope burn. "Lynched for no crime but being black! We've suffocated in slave ships, been wrenched from loved ones, toiled till only death gave relief."

Far out across the plain were hundreds of such groups. Each one had a complaint against God for the evil and suffering being permitted in this world.

How lucky God was to live in Heaven, where all was sweetness and light, where there was no weeping, no fear, no hunger, no hatred. Indeed, what did God know about what man had been forced to endure in this world? "After all, God leads a pretty sheltered life," they said.

So each group sent out a leader, chosen because he had suffered the most. There was a Jew, a black, an untouchable from India, an illegitimate, a person from Hiroshima and one from a Siberian slave camp. In the center of the plain, they consulted with each other. At last, they were ready to present their case.

It was rather simple: Before God would be qualified to be their judge, He must endure what they had endured. Their decision was that God should be sentenced to live on earth as a man.

But because He was God, they set certain safeguards to be sure He could not use His divine powers to help Himself:

Let Him be born a Jew.

Let the legitimacy of His birth be doubted so that none will know who is really His father.

Let Him champion a cause so just but so radical that it brought down upon Him the hate, condemnation and eliminating efforts of every major traditional and established religious authority.

Let Him try to describe what no man has ever seen, tasted, heard or smelled. Let Him try to communicate God to men.

Let him be betrayed by His dearest friends. Let him be indicted on false charges and tried before a prejudiced jury and convicted by a cowardly judge.

Let Him see what it is to be terribly alone, completely abandoned by every living thing. Let Him be tortured, and let Him die the most humiliating death with common thieves.

As each leader announced his portion of the sentence, loud murmurs of approval went up from the great throng of people.

When the last had finished pronouncing the sentence, there was a long silence. No one uttered another word. No one moved. For suddenly, all knew—God had already served His sentence.[1]

Not only has God served His sentence (which He never deserved), but He's also served our sentence. Our sin does not have to separate us from the love of God. He sent His Son to redeem us from sin and to claim us as His spiritual bride.

Are you curious to learn more about God's true character and how you can experience life as the bride of Christ? You don't have to be a scholar or theologian to discover such revelations for yourself. All you really need to do is look to God's world and to His Word.

GLIMPSES OF GOD IN NATURE

Have you ever wondered what God is like, only to look up at a starry sky and sense that there's your answer? As you look at those twinkling constellations, do you have any doubt that God is absolutely brilliant? Or maybe you noticed an abundance of golden daffodils growing alongside the highway and realized, *Oh, God is so glorious!* I see glimpses of His beauty in the towering pine trees of East Texas, His strength in the majestic mountains of Colorado, His creativity in the ocean waves that shape the Pacific shoreline. I hear His heart in the laughter of a child and sense His warmth with the rising and setting of the summer sun. One would have to be deaf, dumb, and blind not to recognize our loving Creator in all of creation.

Why did God craft such a wonderful world for us to live in? I believe it is all part of His plan to woo us into recognizing what a masterful artist He truly is and that He paints these masterpieces especially for us.

At his fiftieth birthday party, my friend Peter was presented with an original work of art, a painting of a place in France he had frequented as a child. Everyone at the party gasped at the artist's thoughtfulness in creating such a masterpiece especially for his friend. The artist didn't just pick something up at a store. He didn't just order something out of a catalog. He spent an enormous amount of time, money, and energy to create a gift custom-tailored to touch the recipient's heart.

God also invests an enormous amount of creativity custom-tailoring gifts that touch our hearts. Imagine something you consider your favorite (your favorite animal, your favorite season, your favorite color...), and realize it is a glorious gift from a God who knows your tastes better than you know them yourself. He designed the scarlet feathers of a cardinal long before I ever knew it was my favorite bird. He formed sugarcane before I ever developed a sweet tooth and crafted the cocoa bean long before I became a raging chocoholic. He inspired the lyrics to my favorite hymns centuries before I'd ever hear them. His world, my world, is overflowing with personal gifts from a personal God who loves me like no other can. Look around your world, and notice how certain aspects of God's creation seem to have your name written on them, as if God is saying, *This is for you, especially from Me.*

Lovers call you today and scorn you tomorrow. Companies follow pay raises with pink slips. Friends applaud you when you drive a classic and dismiss you when you drive a dud. Not God. God is always *"the same" (Psalm 102:27).*

With him "there is no variation or shadow due to change" (James 1:17, ESV).

Catch God in a bad mood? Won't happen. Fear exhausting his grace? A sardine will swallow the Atlantic first. Think he's given up on you? Wrong. Did he not make a promise to you? "God is not a human being, and he does not change his mind. What he says he will do, he does. What he promises, he makes come true" (Numbers 23:19, NCV). He's never sullen or sour, sulking or stressed. His strength, truth, ways, and love never change. He is "the same yesterday and today and forever" (Hebrews 13:8, ESV). And because he is, the Lord "will be the stability of your times" (Isaiah 33:6, NKJV).

—MAX LUCADO, *It's Not About Me*

God often reveals Himself to me through His world on my daily walks. I've always sensed His presence whenever I'm in the outdoors, but several years ago I began feeling as if He were truly walking beside me each time, almost as if He were there in the flesh, holding my hand and conversing with me all along the way.

One crisp fall afternoon, I was walking down a country road, singing "The Power of Your Love" with my arms stretched wide, feeling particularly stirred by the lyrics "As I wait, I'll rise up like the eagle…" I sensed the Lord lifting my head, as if to say, *Look into the sky.* At that precise moment, an eagle was flying directly overhead with outstretched wings (just as my arms were), soaring effortlessly. I knew God was telling me, *I see you worshiping Me with all your heart. I will continue to raise you up like the eagle. Soar! I'm the wind beneath your wings.*

On another day I was walking alongside the Youth With A Mission (YWAM) campus on a country road that bordered their land. I had never walked this particular road before but felt drawn in that direction once I had stepped out of the car in the YWAM parking lot. I had been feeling somewhat distanced from God, but I was also experiencing a deep longing to feel His intimate presence once again. I began to pray, *Lord, I'm embarrassed to even ask You this, but will You give me a reminder of Your love for me? I know Your love never changes, but will You remind me what it feels like to know beyond a shadow of a doubt that I am Your beloved?* As I continued to walk further down the road, I noticed white spray paint covering much of the road ahead and spanning about a tenth of a mile or so. As I got closer, I recognized the first white mark as a *W*…then an *I*…followed by *L L.* My heart leaped when I realized that all these white markings added up to WILL YOU MARRY ME?

Obviously, someone had written out a marriage proposal and perhaps flown his girlfriend over the area to pop the question. *The proposal wasn't even meant for you!* Satan whispered in my mind. But then the Lord reminded me, *I guided you here to this road where you've never walked before, knowing exactly what you'd see when you walked down it. It may have been written by another's hand, but it comes from My heart. You are My beloved, Shannon.* I'll cherish that particular walk until the day I die.

God frequently reminds me on our walks together of my status as His beloved. Right around Christmastime last year, I was reflecting on how God must love me like crazy, and my heart was overflowing with passion and joy. I was singing as loudly as I could a song by Darlene Zschech about how "I'm living under the kiss of heaven..." Suddenly I sensed God saying, *Hey, whoa! Don't miss this. I've got a Christmas present just for you, Shannon. Look up.* I looked up, and the gigantic tree I just "happened" to be passing under, which was completely bare of leaves, had dangling from its bare branches huge clumps of mistletoe. I looked all around and didn't see another tree like it anywhere. Butterflies swarmed in my stomach as I envisioned Jesus standing over me with mistletoe dangling above my head with great anticipation on His face that I would allow Him to grant me His kiss from heaven. I puckered up and blew Him the biggest kiss I possibly could, and I envisioned His face beaming over my sentiment. If I could have done a triple backflip without breaking my neck, I'd have done one at that moment.

GLIMPSES OF GOD IN HUMAN NATURE

Of course, earthly nature isn't the only place we can catch glimpses of God. We can also recognize Him in much of human nature, for we are made in God's image (see Genesis 1:26). When we experience the wide variety of positive emotions that people are capable of, we must remember that God is the source of such emotions. We can only fully experience love because God *is* love...joy, because God *is* joy...peace, because God *is* peace.

As I began writing this book, I was counseling a woman who was experiencing romantic feelings for a particular man. She asked, "Why did God create us in such a way that we have physiological responses to our emotions? Why do thoughts of this guy cause butterflies in my stomach? Why does my heart skip a beat when he looks at me? Why do I get all giddy inside when this guy pays attention to me?"

In that moment I caught another magnificent glimpse of our loving God. He said to me, *I created humans to respond that way to love so they would know how I feel when they turn their attentions toward Me!* I pondered this for a split second, wondering, *God, do You really feel that way when I turn my thoughts toward You?* He affirmed, *Every time you lift your hands in prayer or lift your heart in worship or turn your attentions to Me for any reason at all, I get giddy over you, Shannon.* I shared the revelation with the woman I was talking to, and her response was equivalent to mine. We were both astounded over the idea that God's heart does flip-flops when our attentions turn toward Him.

While creation and human nature can help us understand who God is, one of the clearest glimpses of God comes from reading the love letter He wrote to us.

GLIMPSES OF GOD IN HIS LOVE LETTER

Sometimes we are lulled into thinking that it's really not that important to read God's Word, as if it simply contains historical information that doesn't apply to us today. Let me ask you this: If your husband or boyfriend wrote you a love letter and handed it to you, how eager would you be to open it? How long would it take your eyes to devour every word of it? Would it seem urgent? Would you make it an immediate priority? Remember that the Bible is God's love letter to you, written straight from His heart in order to touch yours.

We tend to forget this, if we ever understood it at all. We lose sight of the immense value of the Scriptures. We grab them if we need them, but otherwise they just sit there. If we leave our Bibles buried in the bookshelves or collecting dust on our bedside tables, God's words will never come alive to us.

When I was a little girl, I couldn't grasp this truth. I assumed I was a good Christian because I went to church, put my quarters in the offering plate, and allowed my Sunday-school teachers to spoon-feed me a Bible story and a memory verse or two. The contents of Scripture were little more than tissue-paper pages filled with stories of flannel-graph characters who didn't seem to have anything to do with real life, at least not my life. So even after the car accident, my Bible initially went unread and my life went unchanged. I was alive, but I wasn't really living. I continued looking for love in all the wrong places, rather than seeking to understand God's lavish love for me.

I experienced a turning point in a small church singles group when we lost our regular teacher. Rather than disband the class, we agreed we'd take turns teaching the lessons. Back then, I was too ignorant to know just how ignorant I was about God's Word. I felt like I could probably wing it, so I volunteered along with everyone else. As my Sunday to teach approached, I began fumbling through pages of my Bible, wondering what topic I could possibly present. Sure, I knew many of the biblical characters, but did I really know why those stories were in the Bible or what they were trying to teach? I realized that in most cases I didn't. I was in over my head, but rather than go down without a fight, I decided to ask God to help me mine the riches that are deep inside the Bible. I asked Him to reveal Himself to me in a way that I had never known before.

God can't resist such a prayer. He lit a fire in my bones, not just to read His words or study them, but to truly live them out and recognize how precious and applicable they are to my life. I was inspired to reach in and grab hold of His timeless truths as never before, so they would bring a greater sense of life to my soul. I began seeing His Word as the most eloquently written love letter I could ever imagine, and I got giddy over the idea that God knew me intimately and loved me extravagantly. Here are some of my favorite passages:

> For you created my inmost being;
>> you knit me together in my mother's womb.
> I praise you because I am fearfully and wonderfully made;
>> your works are wonderful,
>> I know that full well.
> My frame was not hidden from you
>> when I was made in the secret place.
> When I was woven together in the depths of the earth,
>> your eyes saw my unformed body.
> All the days ordained for me
>> were written in your book
>> before one of them came to be.
>
> How precious to me are your thoughts, O God!
>> How vast is the sum of them!
> Were I to count them,
>> they would outnumber the grains of sand.
>>> (Psalm 139:13–18, NIV)

"For I know the plans I have for you," declares the LORD, "plans to prosper you and not to harm you, plans to give you hope and a future." (Jeremiah 29:11, NIV)

> Your unfailing love, O LORD, is as vast as the heavens;
>> your faithfulness reaches beyond the clouds.
>> Your righteousness is like the mighty mountains,
>>> your justice like the ocean depths.

> You care for people and animals alike, O LORD.
>> How precious is your unfailing love, O God!
> All humanity finds shelter
>> in the shadow of your wings.
> You feed them from the abundance of your own house,
>> letting them drink from your rivers of delight.
>> (Psalm 36:5–8)

> The LORD your God is with you,
>> he is mighty to save.
> He will take great delight in you,
>> he will quiet you with his love,
>> he will rejoice over you with singing. (Zephaniah 3:17, NIV)

As I began reading God's love letter more and more, He showed me something of myself in almost every Bible character I read about. But even more important, God began showing me how He had worked in their lives, and I experienced a hunger for Him to work in my life too. I sensed Him calling me to take some major leaps of faith, leaps that formerly would have caused me to cower in retreat out of fear. God began wooing and pursuing me into taking His hand and following Him in faith.

GLIMPSES OF GOD IN THE OLD TESTAMENT

While I have many Old Testament favorites, the character I've identified with most (aside from Moses) is Abram (later renamed Abraham). Abraham is considered the "father of the Jews" because God chose him in order to establish a separate nation (Israel) that would be His "chosen people"— chosen to demonstrate to the world the wonders of their magnificent and almighty God. In Genesis 12:2–3 God says to Abram:

I will cause you to become the father of a great nation. I will bless you and make you famous, and I will make you a blessing to others. I will bless those who bless you and curse those who curse you. All the families of the earth will be blessed through you.

But God required something of Abram first—an act of obedience and trust. He called Abram to move to an entirely new and completely unfamiliar land, which required an enormous leap of faith for Abram and his entire household. When I first read this story, I had no idea how closely my own life would come to resemble it.

In 1998 after several months of trying to break free from an inappropriate emotional entanglement with a ministry colleague, I was on my way to a four-day sabbatical to Lake Palestine with a female pastor friend. We missed our exit and accidentally wound up in the unfamiliar city of Lindale, Texas. It was lunchtime, so we grabbed some burritos. As Pam was saying grace, I sensed God saying, *Move here.*

What's in Lindale? I kept wondering for the next two days. I finally called my husband from Lake Palestine and said, "I think I heard God telling me we should move to Lindale, Texas, but I know Dallas is your home, so if you'll just tell me I'm crazy and that it's not going to happen, perhaps I'll be able to concentrate on what I came here to do."

"I won't tell you that you're crazy," Greg replied, "but I will pray about it."

When I got home two days later, Greg had the van all packed and the kids dressed and ready. "Where are we going?" I asked my "never-have-done-a-spontaneous-thing-in-life" husband.

"We're going to Lindale!" Greg replied with a smile and a wink.

As we prayed about how God was leading us in this matter, we were drawn to Genesis 12:1, where the Lord said to Abram, "Leave your country, your relatives, and your father's house, and go to the land that I will show you." We decided to throw out a fleece. We stuck a For Sale by

Owner sign in our front yard and asked $25,000 more for our house than we had paid for it three years earlier. It sold within six days, and the buyer insisted we be out within three weeks. We called an East Texas Realtor and said, "You have to find us a house in Lindale, and fast!"

Just two days prior, a rustic log cabin home overlooking a creek on 122 acres of land was placed on the market. We immediately made an offer and found ourselves moving to Lindale, not having any idea why, other than that God was directing us there. We soon met our neighbors, a campus called Teen Mania Ministries, where I would quickly find my niche ministering to college-age women who have a tendency to look for love in all the wrong places, just as I had when I was their age. Shortly after our move, Greg was asked to serve as the chief financial officer at another neighboring missionary campus called Mercy Ships International.

We had no doubt that God knew what He was doing when Pam and I missed the exit that day and wound up in Lindale, Texas. The log cabin we purchased had sat vacant for over ten years, but the owner hadn't placed it on the market until the very week we began looking for a home to buy in Lindale. We felt as if God had been holding it in reserve for us, waiting for the exact moment when we would be open to His leading us to move there. Had we not been willing, as Abram was, to obediently venture away from our Dallas roots, we would have never discovered this "promised land" that we call Cross Creek.

But as much as we love our secluded log cabin home, the beautiful woods, rolling hills, our friendly community, and the opportunities we have to serve the Lord in our respective ministries, we know that the greatest reward of our obedience is simply a more intimate relationship with the One who called us here. We can frequently hear God saying, as He did to Abram in Genesis 15:1, "I am your shield, your very great reward" (NIV).

At some point, God may call you out of your comfort zone as well. If He does, remember what my pastor always says: "God does not ask of us that which does not ultimately benefit us." Regardless of what kind of change God asks of you, and no matter how difficult what He asks may seem, obedience to His voice will always result in blessing in the long run. That's just the kind of God we serve. He wants to give us marvelous things and experiences that we perhaps never dreamed of, but first we have to let go of our own little world and begin to venture out into His.

I have another scriptural soul mate who also discovered the Lord to be her very great reward— the woman at the well.

GLIMPSES OF GOD IN THE NEW TESTAMENT

In the fourth chapter of John's gospel, we see how Jesus bucked the social pecking order when He went out of His way to speak privately with a Samaritan woman. He could see this gal was thirsty, not just for the water found in the well, but for living water found only in the Messiah. He didn't mince words as He lovingly reminded her that she'd had five hus-bands and was now living with a man she wasn't married to.

Standing spiritually naked before Him, she recognizes Jesus must be a prophet, but then He takes the blinders off her eyes when He reveals Himself as one who can offer what her soul longs for most. You see, Jesus knew He was the only one who could provide the love that continued to elude this woman, relationship after relationship. He knew she was thirsty for something real. He wanted to satisfy her in a way that no other man possibly could, so He offered her living water so she would never have to go thirsty again. What woman doesn't want that?

As I began in the spring of 2000 to create what would be the first of many books addressing female sexuality, I had a clear vision of what my first work should be titled—*Words of Wisdom for Women at the Well: Quenching Your Heart's Thirst for Love and Intimacy.* However, had I never dug through Scripture and mined the precious treasures from the story of the woman at the well, I would never have been inspired to write such a book, or perhaps any other book. I saw myself in the woman at the well, and I saw God's merciful heart in His loving response to her.

WOOED AND PURSUED BETWEEN THE PAGES OF SCRIPTURE

Perhaps you want to deepen your relationship with God, but it hasn't occurred to you that the best way to do this is by simply allowing Him to give you glimpses into His character through His Word. As you read the Bible, are you inviting Him to help you identify with the characters written about in the Scriptures? Are you looking to see how God has wooed and pursued humanity into a love relationship with Him? In the book *Biblical Preaching*, Haddon Robinson explains how we can approach God's Word so we can get the most from it:

> God reveals Himself in the Scriptures. The Bible, therefore, isn't a textbook about ethics or a manual on how to solve personal problems. The Bible is a book about God. When you study a biblical text, therefore, you should ask, "What is the vision of God in this passage?" God is always there. Look for Him. At different times He is the Creator, a good Father, the Redeemer, a rejected Lover, a Husband, a King, a Savior, a Warrior, a Judge, a Reaper, a vineyard Keeper, a banquet Host, a Fire, a Hen protecting her chicks, and so on....
>
> Not only is it important to look for the vision of God in a passage, but you will also want to look at the human factor. How should people in the biblical text have responded to this vision of God? How *did* they respond? Should this vision of God have made any practical difference in their lives? This human factor is the condition that men and women today have in common with

the characters in the Bible. The human factor may show up in sins such as rebellion, unbelief, adultery, greed, laziness, selfishness, or gossip. It may also show up in people puzzling about the human condition as a result of sickness, grief, anxiety, doubt, trials, or the sense that God has misplaced their names and addresses. It is this human factor that usually prompted the prophets and apostles to speak or write what they did.[2]

The Bible is a book written for us today. It may have originated centuries ago, but its truths are timeless treasures that we desperately need to apply to our own lives. While God is eager to reveal these treasures to us, we must open our Bibles to recognize them. They are like precious gems waiting to be mined out of the rough crust of the earth. In fact, the Hebrew word for *Bible* is *mikra,* which means "the calling out of God."[3] God is calling out to us from the Scriptures, telling us that He wants to be known and loved by us, just as He knows and loves us.

The more familiar we are with Scripture, the more confidence we will have that we are hearing God correctly as He speaks to us. For a unique and enlightening devotional experience, hide your Bible somewhere in the house for one week and pretend you live in a country where Bibles are forbidden. During your private devotions, try creating your own Bible from memory by writing down as many scriptures as you can recall. This is a great way to test your knowledge of God's Word and to be encouraged by just how many verses you have truly hidden in your heart, for that is where they become a powerful weapon against temptation. Consider trying this every couple of years to see how much your knowledge of the Word has increased.

Don't settle for just reciting a few memory verses or listening to a weekly sermon. We must *encounter God* in the pages of the Bible. The difference between being spoon-fed a Bible story versus witnessing it come

TEN TIPS FOR UNDERSTANDING GOD'S WORD

While entire books have been written and ministries formed around the science and art of properly interpreting the Bible, here are ten questions that you can ask yourself to better understand God's Word.

1. Who is the writer of this passage, and who was the audience?*

2. What were the historical or cultural circumstances that prompted the author to write what he did?*

3. What did the author say in the chapters and verses just prior to and after this passage? How does the passage "fit" into the bigger picture of what the author is saying?

4. Consider the general literary form and how the author intended his words to be understood. For example, poetry (such as the Psalms) is usually interpreted figuratively, whereas prose (such as the gospels of Matthew, Mark, Luke, and John) is interpreted literally, and apocalyptic literature (such as Daniel and Revelation) is interpreted symbolically.

5. Are there particular words you need to look up or research to find their true definitions?**

6. Ask, "What can I learn about God from this passage? Where is He, and what is He really doing in this situation?"

7. Ask, "What can I learn about human nature from this passage? Is this character responding appropriately or inappropriately to what God is doing in this story?"

8. Determine what principle we need to learn from this passage of Scripture. What is the heart of the message that the author was trying to express?

9. Determine if the principle needs to be translated to our modern culture. For example, to "greet one another with a holy kiss" (Romans 16:16; 1 Corinthians 16:20; 2 Corinthians 13:12; 1 Thessalonians 5:26, NIV) may have been fine in that culture, but in our modern culture it might be considered inappropriate to kiss everyone we meet. The scriptures could be understood today as, "greet one another with a hearty handshake." The idea is that we greet one another warmly, not the form of greeting we use.

10. Compare your analysis with the analyses of others to make sure you understand the passage correctly.***

---

*   In most study Bibles, this information can be found in the introductory pages just prior to each book.

** Many books and Web sites can help you research a word's meaning. For example: www.crosswalk.com, www.bible.org, or www.biblegateway.com.

*** You can use a variety of Bible commentaries to compare your findings with others'. My personal favorite is the abridged edition of *The Expositor's Bible Commentary* by Kenneth L. Barker and John R. Kohlenberger III (Grand Rapids, MI: Zondervan, 2004).

alive in our hearts, minds, and spirits is like the difference between read-ing a book on poverty versus standing in line at a soup kitchen with a homeless mother and her five hungry children. There is a life-changing difference between knowing *about* God and knowing and experiencing God personally.

If you want to understand who God is, get into His Word. There you will begin to understand who you are in light of His grace. Learn to live the Word, breathe it, chew on it, digest it, and allow it to nourish the core of your soul. Allow it to change you from the inside out.

Learn to see glimpses of God's nature as you look around at the breathtaking splendor of His creation. Know that He fashioned this world with you in mind. As other humans inspire heart-warming emotions in you, give glory to the God in whose image we are made. Open His love letter to you, and approach each day with great anticipation of what God will do in you and through you. Inhale His revelations, let their sweet aroma intoxicate you, and allow the Creator to woo you and pursue you until you become completely His.

An Extraordinary Proposal

When my daughter, Erin, was a preschooler, she had a most ardent admirer in our neighborhood play group. For over two years, her friend Solomon followed her around everywhere and showered her with his attentions and affections. His outspoken adoration created many sweet, innocent, and truly unforgettable moments in the Ethridge history books.

One day as we were walking Solomon back to his house down the street, Erin ran way ahead of us. Solomon yelled out, "Erin! STOP—In the Name of Love!" (a song his mom frequently sang around the house). On another day Solomon brought Erin a fresh bouquet of flowers, explaining, "I brought you these pink tulips because they reminded me of your pink two lips!" (Yes, we got quite the chuckle out of that one). Convinced that he and Erin would marry someday, four-year-old Solomon declared his intentions by insisting, "Erin, you are a girl, and when you grow up, you are going to be a woman. And I'm a boy, and when I grow up, I'm going to be a man. And when we grow up, I want to marry you, and we're gonna have a hundred kids, okay?" Clueless as to what challenges parenting such a crew would bring, or even the biological impossibilities of such a dream, Erin just smiled and sweetly responded, "Okay!"

Sadly, the day eventually came when Solomon had to move to California. Driving home from our last play date together, he said, "Oh, Erin, I wish you could move to California with me, and we could have bunk beds!" I'm not sure who cried more the day he moved—Erin, Solomon, or me.

While Erin's attitudes about love and marriage have definitely matured now that she's growing up, her conversations with Solomon gave me great insight into the heart of a young girl. One of the first and most fervent dreams she carries in her heart is to love, be loved, and to eventually marry the man of her dreams. It was no different for me growing up, and while I can't say it's a universal female phenomenon, I think it's safe to say that most women long to be admired and desired by a wonderful man.

Well, guess what? The most wonderful man who ever walked the planet has got you in His sights, girlfriend, and He's got marriage on His mind. In case you don't believe me, let me take you to the Last Supper, where Jesus made this extraordinary proposal.

The First Last Supper

The night before Jesus was crucified, He gathered His twelve disciples in an upper room, where they experienced the origin of a sacred tradition we call "taking communion." I remember approaching the communion table as a little girl, eager to taste the fresh bread and sweet grape juice that the ushers offered. The preacher said the communion elements represented Jesus' body, "which was broken for me," and Jesus' blood, "which was shed for the remission of my sins." That sounded good enough to me. For many years I partook of communion with this limited knowledge of what was taking place in the spiritual realm.

But several years ago, I saw a video series produced by Focus on the Family and narrated by biblical scholar Ray Vander Laan called *That the*

World May Know. In one of the videos, Vander Laan explains that in biblical times a bride-to-be had a say in whether she would marry her potential groom. After he had negotiated a bride price for her (we'll talk more about bride price later), the groom would seek her approval of the arrangement by pouring a cup of wine and handing it to her. By this act, he was saying, "I offer you my life."

At that moment, the potential bride had a decision to make. If she did not care to marry the man, she could refuse the cup. The negotiations would come to a halt, and the young man would return home, rejected. But if she was willing to marry him, she would take the cup and drink from it. By her actions, she was saying, "I receive your life, and I give you mine in return." Then preparations would begin for a wedding celebration, which included the groom's returning to his father's house to build an additional room where the marriage would eventually be consummated.

With these traditions in mind, let's return to the Last Supper. When Jesus handed the cup of wine to each of His disciples that night, He was saying, in essence, "Will you marry Me? Will you be My spiritual bride?" At that moment His followers had a decision to make. They could reject the cup and refuse Jesus' spiritual marriage proposal, or they could drink from it, receiving His life and offering theirs to Him in return.

Once they drank from the cup, Jesus explained that He was going away and that they couldn't come with Him. The disciples were bewildered, but Jesus responded, "Don't be troubled. You trust God, now trust in me. There are many rooms in my Father's home, and I am going to prepare a place for you. If this were not so, I would tell you plainly. When everything is ready, I will come and get you, so that you will always be with me where I am" (John 14:1–3).

Jesus was referring to the Jewish tradition of the groom's going to prepare a place for his bride that adjoined his father's house. He was saying, "I am going to my Father's house to prepare the wedding chamber, where

WHAT DOES THE BIBLE SAY
ABOUT THE BRIDE OF CHRIST?[1]

In the Old Testament, God's covenant with Israel is commonly pictured as a marriage pledge, with Israel as God's bride.

- Through the prophet Jeremiah, the Lord said to Israel, "I remember the devotion of your youth, your love as a bride" (Jeremiah 2:2, RSV). He went on to lament the fact that Israel had been faithless; by going after other gods, she had actually prostituted herself and become an adulteress (see Jeremiah 3:6–9, 20).
- The theme of Israel's desertion of her lover (God) was explicitly treated in Ezekiel 16 and in Hosea. The terms *harlotry* and *whoredom* were used to connote disloyalty to Yahweh and allegiance to other gods.
- Through his own struggles with a faithless wife, the prophet Hosea experienced God's agony over His bride, Israel, and His longing for her to return to Him. Hosea was given a vision of a future day in which God would betroth His people to Him forever in steadfast love and faithfulness (see Hosea 2:19–20).

In the New Testament, the bride of Christ is often a metaphor for the church, with Christ pictured as a husband, and the church as His bride.

- John the Baptist saw himself as "the bridegroom's friend" (John 3:29) who, according to Jewish custom, takes care of the wedding arrangements.
- Paul promises the church to Christ, presenting her as a pure bride (see 2 Corinthians 11:2–3). He saw himself as the church's spiritual father (see 1 Corinthians 4:15) and was worried that the young bride (the church) might commit adultery by her willingness to accept "a different Jesus," "a different Spirit," or "a different kind of gospel" (2 Corinthians 11:4).
- In Ephesians 5:22–23, the relationship between Christ and His church is compared to the relationship between a husband and wife. The church's submission to Christ is compared with the wife's submission to the husband, but the focus of the passage is on the role of the husband: he is to love her as Christ loved the church and gave Himself up for her. As the man's love for his wife intends her wholeness, so Christ's love of the church intends her completeness.
- The vision in Revelation 19:7–8 announces the marriage of the Lamb (Christ) to the bride (the church). In Revelation 21 (ESV) the vision depicts the new Jerusalem coming down from heaven, "prepared as a bride adorned for her husband" (verse 2). Then the seer is invited to behold "the Bride, the wife of the Lamb" (verse 9) and to see the holy city "coming down out of heaven from God" (verse 10). The new Jerusalem is identified as the people of God, the bride of Christ, among whom and with whom God will be present forever.

we will one day consummate our love for one another and enjoy each other's presence throughout all eternity." Jesus was telling His disciples—and you and me—that He was returning to His Father's house in order to prepare a place for each one of us, for we are all His beloved bride (see the sidebar on page 36).

I don't know about you, but I find it unfathomable that the God of the universe would make me such an offer, particularly when I consider that He knows my tendency toward unfaithfulness.

AN UNFAITHFUL BRIDE

Imagine a groom standing at the altar, watching his lovely bride glide down the aisle to pledge herself to him in holy matrimony. Dreams swirl in his head of putting the ring on her finger, taking her in his arms on their honeymoon, and spending the rest of his life with her by his side.

Do you think this groom would go through with the wedding if he knew his bride would be unfaithful to him, prostituting herself with other men and treating their wedding vows with about as much respect as one might treat the weekly trash? Would he still marry her if he knew she would be unfaithful to him?

Would you make such a commitment if the tables were turned and you knew the person you were about to marry had quite the dark past, a past that would definitely repeat itself? Or would you consider it more reasonable to pass on this opportunity and seek a more qualified candidate down the road, one who would be faithful to you forever?

Now imagine for a moment that you are that unfaithful bride. When your groom is asked if he will love, honor, and cherish you forever, even though he knows you will give yourself to others, what will he say? Do you expect him to say, "I do," or is this reason enough for him to say, "I don't think so!"?

It's hard to imagine that a groom would commit himself to an unfaithful bride, but this is exactly what God has done with you and me. In fact, many theologians and scholars agree that the Old Testament story of Hosea and Gomer is a picture of God's relationship with His spiritual bride.

In this Old Testament book, God calls the prophet Hosea to take Gomer as his wife even though she's an adulteress. Similarly, God takes His bride, the nation of Israel (and ultimately us, the church) in spite of our unfaithfulness. Let's turn to the story and read of God's unreasonably passionate pursuit of His beloved bride.

> "I will punish her for all the times she deserted me, when she burned incense to her images of Baal, put on her earrings and jewels, and went out looking for her lovers," says the LORD.
>
> "But then I will win her back once again. I will lead her out into the desert and speak tenderly to her there. I will return her vineyards to her and transform the Valley of Trouble into a gateway of hope. She will give herself to me there, as she did long ago when she was young, when I freed her from her captivity in Egypt.
>
> "In that coming day," says the LORD, "you will call me 'my husband' instead of 'my master.' O Israel, I will cause you to forget your images of Baal; even their names will no longer be spoken.... I will make you my wife forever, showing you righteousness and justice, unfailing love and compassion. I will be faithful to you and make you mine, and you will finally know me as LORD." (Hosea 2:13–17, 19–20)

Without question, I find this to be one of the most extraordinary and comforting passages in the Bible. Why? Because I, like Gomer, have been an incredibly unfaithful bride. Perhaps I've never invoked the name of

Baal, but I've been seduced by plenty of other gods, gods such as greed, selfishness, pride, and sexual immorality. If I examine how I've spent significant blocks of time over the years, I'd also have to say that I've bowed down to many other petty gods—the television, the telephone, inappropriate relationships, the computer and Internet, and shopping—in my futile efforts to satisfy my soul. After all, the essence of idolatry is looking to something or someone else to fill us up and satisfy us in a way that only our Creator God can.

None of us are faithful to our Bridegroom—not one—but He has known this about each of us all along. The Bible is filled with unfaithful brides, from Adam and Abraham in the Old Testament to Peter and Paul in the New Testament. Yet these sin stories often turn out to be success stories of how God cleansed these individuals and called them His own. He can do the same for us. In fact, God, in His loving kindness, has already taken care of the necessary wedding arrangements in order to make good on His extraordinary proposal. What arrangements am I referring to? Two in particular—the payment of the bride price and the provision of the wedding garments.

PAYMENT OF THE BRIDE PRICE

In ancient times, a suitor was expected to pay the bride's family a hefty price in order to receive her hand in marriage. The most familiar examples of this tradition come from the stories in the Old Testament about Jacob (with Rachel) and David (with Michal). In each of these stories, the father of the bride established or agreed to the bride price, and the groom paid the price without hesitation. In fact, both Jacob and David went above and beyond the agreed-upon price because of their love for their chosen brides.

In Genesis 29 we see that Jacob falls in love with Rachel, Laban's younger daughter, and offers to work seven years without pay in exchange for her hand in marriage. In verses 20–21 we read:

So Jacob spent the next seven years working to pay for Rachel. But his love for her was so strong that it seemed to him but a few days. Finally, the time came for him to marry her. "I have fulfilled my contract," Jacob said to Laban. "Now give me my wife so we can be married."

Unfortunately, Laban had a cruel trick up his sleeve. Rather than giving Rachel to Jacob, he sent her older sister, Leah, into Jacob's dark room instead. The next morning, Jacob was shocked and dismayed to find that rather than consummating his love with Rachel, he had experienced sexual relations with his intended sister-in-law! However, Jacob's love for Rachel led him to make yet another deal with his tricky father-in-law.

So Jacob agreed to work seven more years [for Rachel]. A week after Jacob had married Leah, Laban gave him Rachel, too.... So Jacob slept with Rachel, too, and he loved her more than Leah. He then stayed and worked the additional seven years. (verses 28, 30)

Can you imagine loving someone so much that you'd commit to working full-time for fourteen years (without pay!) just to marry him? To realize what a sacrifice this would require, do the math. If a man who earned an annual salary of $50,000 made this kind of sacrifice today, he would be paying the equivalent of $700,000 for his bride. Yet, to Jacob, the years he invested seemed "but a few days" because of his unwavering love for Rachel.

David experienced a similar above-and-beyond kind of love for Michal, but unfortunately he also had to deal with an underhanded father-in-law. King Saul was delighted to discover that his daughter had fallen in love with David because Saul saw it as an opportunity to lure David into a deathtrap. Saul instructed his men to sweet-talk David into believing he was well liked by the king, hoping to coax David into accepting Saul's invitation to become his son-in-law. However, David knew he could not afford the bride price of a king's daughter. Still, Saul was determined to lead David into danger.

> When Saul's men reported [David's response] back to the king, he told them, "Tell David that all I want for the bride price is one hundred Philistine foreskins! Vengeance on my enemies is all I really want." But what Saul had in mind was that David would be killed in the fight.
>
> David was delighted to accept the offer. So before the time limit expired, he and his men went out and killed two hundred Philistines and presented all their foreskins to the king. So Saul gave Michal to David to be his wife. (1 Samuel 18:24–27)

David wasn't one to do the minimum. He doubled the mileage required. He provided two hundred foreskins instead of one hundred. David's love for Michal inspired such fervor that he thought nothing of the bride price.

Just as Jacob's and David's love compelled them to do whatever it took to acquire their chosen brides, Jesus Christ did the same for us, His spiritual bride. Keep in mind that Jesus wasn't simply negotiating the price for one individual, but for all individuals, for all eternity. So what price did He pay? No amount of money could possibly have made that kind of purchase. The price had to be exorbitant. It had to cost Him everything. And it did. It cost Him His life. Yet He paid the price willingly.

Just hours before He died, Jesus fell face down on the ground in the Garden of Gethsemane and prayed, "My Father! If it is possible, *let this cup of suffering* be taken away from me. Yet I want your will, not mine" (Matthew 26:39). The price being demanded of Him was difficult to submit to, but Jesus agreed to submit nonetheless. He demonstrated His willingness to pay the price a second time when He scolded Peter for cutting off the right ear of the soldier who tried to arrest Him. Jesus said to Peter, "Put your sword back into its sheath. Shall I not *drink from the cup* the Father has given me?" (John 18:10–11).

> From Jesus' words "Whoever loves Me..." and "Do you love Me?" we sense how much He yearns for us to love Him. But it is a special kind of love He seeks. It is the love that is reflected in the relationship between an earthly bride and her bridegroom. An exclusive love. A love that tolerates no rivals. A love that gives the beloved, the bridegroom, the first place. As the heavenly Bridegroom, Jesus lays claim to such first love. Because He loves us so dearly, He longs to have the whole of us. Jesus gave Himself unreservedly for us. Now He yearns for us to give ourselves completely to Him, with all that we are and have, so that He can truly be our first love.
>
> —BASILEA SCHLINK, *My All for Him*

Jesus paid a high price for each one of us. He drank the cup. He offered His very life to purchase His beloved spiritual bride, to purchase you and me. I wonder, what will you do with the communion cup next time it is offered to you? Knowing that it is not just a sip of wine or grape juice, but a symbol of Jesus' marriage proposal, will you refuse it? Or will you drink it, accepting His proposal and offering your life to Him in return? Will you agree to embrace your role as His spiritual bride?

If you said yes, you'll be happy to hear that Jesus has also purchased your wedding dress.

ISN'T IT JUST A JEWISH THING?

When I began studying about the bride-of-Christ analogy and what it means for us as individuals, I faced some opposition. Every once in a while, a well-meaning person would say, "We are not the bride of Christ. Only Israel is considered the bride of Christ." Those who subscribe to this theory perhaps see little or no correlation between the God of the Old Testament and the God of the New Testament. Thus Jews are believed to be the "bride" of Christ while Gentiles (everyone who isn't a Jew) simply got saved from hell, but aren't included in any of the spiritual promises made to the nation of Israel.

As Gentiles, we hold no claim to the promise made to the Israelites for a particular parcel of land (known as the Promised Land), but we certainly inherit all of the spiritual promises made by God, including that of being the bride of Christ. Consider the following words of Paul:

> Since Abraham and the other patriarchs were holy, their children will also be holy. For if the roots of the tree are holy, the branches will be, too.
>
> But some of these branches from Abraham's tree, some of the Jews, have been broken off. And you Gentiles, who were branches from a wild olive tree, were grafted in. So now you *also receive the blessing God has promised Abraham and his children,* sharing in God's rich nourishment of his special olive tree. (Romans 11:16–17)

Of course, we do not inherit all of the spiritual blessings God promised Israel simply because we are Gentiles. We inherit them when we embrace God's plan of salvation and become Gentile believers. Earlier in the book of Romans, Paul explains:

> If the Gentiles obey God's law, won't God give them all the rights and honors of being his own people? In fact, uncircumcised Gentiles who keep God's law will be much better off than you Jews who are circumcised and know so much about God's law but don't obey it. (Romans 2:26–27)

In other words, if your heart is right with God, you are considered part of the corporate bride of Christ, regardless of whether you are a Jew or a Gentile. Besides, Paul declares that in Christ there is no longer a distinction between the two:

> There is no longer Jew or Gentile, slave or free, male or female. For you are all Christians—you are one in Christ Jesus. And now that you belong to Christ, you are the true children of Abraham. You are his heirs and now all the promises God gave to him belong to you. (Galatians 3:28–29)

I don't think it can be made any clearer. We are all invited into an intimate love relationship with Jesus, regardless of our heritage, our social status, or our gender. All that is required is that we submit to Him as our heavenly Bridegroom and love Him with a bridal love.

Provision of the Wedding Garments

One day as Greg and I were making our wedding arrangements, I begged him to go with me to a bridal shop and watch me try on dresses. I know, I know…the groom isn't supposed to see the bride in her dress until the wedding day. I didn't intend to buy a dress at that particular shop on that particular day. I just wanted to get his opinion on the styles of dresses that he liked and disliked. I didn't want to walk down the aisle with him thinking, *Oh, my! Why did she pick that dress?*

We walked into the store, and the attendant gathered a dozen or so dresses of varying styles for me to try on. I walked out of the dressing room wearing the first dress, a candlelight-white Alyssa gown adorned in crystal beads across the chest, shoulders, and train. At over $2,000, it was way out of my price range, but I wanted to get Greg's response to the style, so I walked out wearing it just to see his reaction. No amount of preparation could have readied me for the stunned look on his face.

"*That's* the gown, Shannon!' he insisted.

"No, it can't be 'the gown,' Greg! You can't see me in it, and I can't afford this one anyway!" I replied.

I tried on the other eleven dresses, but every time I walked out, Greg just shook his head from side to side and said, "Nope. The first one is it."

I left the bridal shop more discouraged than encouraged. Even if I decided to break tradition and wear the gown Greg had already seen me in, I simply couldn't afford it.

However, two days later Greg showed up at my apartment with a card saying, "Shannon, if you will allow me, I'd really like to buy you that dress as my wedding gift to you." He knew I couldn't afford to buy the dress, but he could, so he did.

Hasn't God done the same for each of us? He knew we could never purchase our own garments for the wedding supper of the Lamb, but He could, so He did.

Perhaps you are wondering, *what is the wedding supper of the Lamb?* In Revelation 19:6–7, John paints a vivid picture of a feast, celebrating the union of Christ and His collective bride.

> Then I heard again what sounded like the shout of a huge crowd, or the roar of mighty ocean waves, or the crash of loud thunder: "Hallelujah! For the Lord our God, the Almighty, reigns. Let us be glad and rejoice and honor him. For the time has come for the wedding feast of the Lamb."

However, according to Jesus we can't come to the wedding supper of the Lamb without the proper garments. He told the disciples:

> The Kingdom of Heaven can be illustrated by the story of a king who prepared a great wedding feast for his son. Many guests were invited, and when the banquet was ready, he sent his servants to notify everyone that it was time to come....
>
> The servants brought in everyone they could find, good and bad alike, and the banquet hall was filled with guests. But when the king came in to meet the guests, he noticed a man who wasn't wearing the proper clothes for a wedding. "Friend," he asked, "how is it that you are here without wedding clothes?" And the man had no reply. Then the king said to his aides, "Bind him hand and foot and throw him out into the outer darkness, where there is weeping and gnashing of teeth." For many are called, but few are chosen. (Matthew 22:2–3; 10–14)

In this parable Jesus was likely telling His disciples, "You can't come to My great wedding feast wearing just anything. You have to be clothed in the proper attire—you have to be clothed in righteousness." And so do we, if we want to attend the wedding supper of the Lamb.

The problem is, we cannot clothe ourselves with the necessary righteousness, regardless of how successful we are in refraining from sin or how many good deeds we manage to squeeze into a day. We can never be good enough. But when Jesus paid the price for us by dying on the cross in our place, the blood He shed canceled our sins and paved our way into the presence of God. He clothed us in His righteousness (see Isaiah 61:10). That's why the passage in Revelation 19 continues:...

> "His bride has prepared herself. She is permitted to wear the finest white linen." (Fine linen represents the good deeds done by the people of God.)
> And the angel said, "Write this: Blessed are those who are invited to the wedding feast of the Lamb." (verses 7–9)

According to these verses, we, the bride, will be "permitted" to wear the finest white linen at the wedding supper of the Lamb. In biblical times linen was an expensive cloth worn by priests and royalty. It symbolized glorification, purity, loyalty, and faithfulness.[2] Because Jesus has clothed us in His righteousness, we can proudly wear white at the wedding feast of the Lamb.

And when we clothe ourselves with the white wedding dress that Christ has purchased for us to wear, we are the fulfillment of all He has dreamed about for us from the beginning.

A PURE AND SPOTLESS BRIDE

Just before I walked down the aisle toward Greg, I had to chase away tormenting thoughts such as, *I just wish I had saved myself for Him! I hate it that I can't give my husband the gift of my virginity like he'll be giving me tonight!* But guess what? At the wedding supper of the Lamb, I'll have absolutely no regrets. All our guilt and shame has been completely washed away by what Christ has already done, and we will know that we are the pure and spotless bride that God intended for His Son.

Consider Paul's words in his letter to the Colossians:

For God was pleased to have all his fullness dwell in [Jesus], and through him to reconcile to himself all things, whether things on earth or things in heaven, by making peace *through his blood, shed on the cross.*

Once you were alienated from God and were enemies in your minds because of your evil behavior. But now he has reconciled you by Christ's physical body through death to present you *holy in his sight, without blemish and free from accusation*— if you continue in your faith, established and firm, not moved from the hope held out in the gospel....

We proclaim him, admonishing and teaching everyone with all wisdom, so that we may present everyone perfect in Christ. (Colossians 1:19–23, 28, NIV)

Perhaps you struggle with feeling less than worthy of God's love because of your unfaithfulness to Him. Perhaps you can't see yourself as a pure and spotless bride. If so, let me gently lift your downcast face and put some light back in your eyes. Did you catch what Paul said? You are *perfect* in Christ. You are *holy* in His sight, without blemish and free from accusation. It doesn't matter that you don't feel worthy, because God's lavish love and unconditional acceptance of you isn't based on your worthiness. It's based on His goodness. It's based on the bride price that His perfect Son already paid for you—and me. We are no longer just anybody. We are His chosen. We are His beloved bride.

We may remember the sins we've committed in the past, but as far as

PREPARATION OF THE BRIDE

Have you ever wondered why John the Baptist invited people down to the Jordan River to be immersed in water as a sign of their faith? Why couldn't he just ask them to shake his hand, or draw a line in the sand, or make some other random sign that they wanted to confirm their belief in the coming Messiah?

John may have been imitating an ancient Jewish wedding tradition called the *mikvah*, a tradition that continues among many Jews. According to this tradition, a bride is required to perform a ritual of fully immersing herself in water prior to her wedding.

Throughout history and into our contemporary age, immersion in a mikvah signifies the "rebirth" and change of status of a convert.[3] In her book, *To Be a Jewish Woman*, Lisa Aiken explains the intimate details of the mikvah even further:

> A *mikvah* is a collection of water emanating from a natural source, such as a spring or rainwater. One reason why a bathtub, Jacuzzi, or swimming pool cannot serve as a *mikvah* is because the water that goes into them is not directly connected to the natural source from which it emanates....
>
> When women immerse, they are not allowed to have even a speck of dirt on them. This is because whenever

we renew our spiritual connections with God and remove
our spiritual blockages, nothing can stand between us and
the Source of all spiritual blessing.

A *mikvah* must contain a certain amount of water.
There must be at least 40 *seah* (a biblical unit of measure)
of water. The number 40 symbolizes the amount of time
(in days) it takes for a fetus to attain human form.... The
mikvah itself represents the womb.[4]

Perhaps some of these details of the mikvah bring other biblical images to mind, such as Jesus' claim in John 4 that He alone
offers us "living water," not stagnant water that has been discon-
nected from its source. And the number forty? How about the
forty days and nights of flooding that Noah and his family
endured—a spiritual "cleansing" of the earth of all the evil which
had become so prevalent? Obviously, the mikvah is an experience
rich with tradition and religious symbolism. It is intended to be a
complete spiritual cleansing and a transition between our spiritual
death and our spiritual life, a special moment when we are spiritually born again as pure and spotless creations.

Could John's intention in baptizing believers in the Jordan
River have been to emulate the mikvah? I believe that, based
on how he called himself "the bridegroom's friend" (John 3:29),
his intention was to prepare us, the bride of Christ, for our wedding day.

God is concerned, we've been justified (meaning "just-as-if-I'd *never* done those things!"). Our sins are no longer held against us. We've been set free. We've been redeemed. Even in our unfaithfulness, Jesus has betrothed Himself to us forever.

HOW WILL WE RESPOND?

It is the most moving and compelling love story of all time—Jesus extending such an extraordinary marriage proposal to us, paying the exorbitantly high price to redeem us, and permitting us to wear white as His pure and spotless bride. But the ending is up to each of us, individually. Will you dismiss what I am saying as some hokey fairy tale? Or will you embrace these truths and give Jesus the response He longs to receive?

4

The Response He
Longs to Receive

Five years into our marriage, Greg and I had dinner at some friends'
house one December evening. I went to bed as soon as we returned
home, feeling exhausted. However, I was suddenly wide awake at 2:00
a.m., unsure why I couldn't go back to sleep. I tossed and turned for a
while, and then my thoughts turned to God. I had not been faithful to
have regular quiet times with Him, so I asked, *Lord, did You wake me up
because You wanted to talk with me?*

I heard a soft rain begin outside my window. As I listened to the unexpected shower, I sensed that I was conversing with God through nature,
so I prayed, *Lord, are You trying to tell me something?* The rain grew
stronger and seemed to be saying that someone was about to die. *Is that
it? Are You trying to tell me someone is going to die?* The sky grumbled
ominously.

I thought, *It's probably my grandfather or grandmother. They are in a
nursing home and getting feeble. It must be one of them.* But then I realized
that God wouldn't wake me up to tell me something I had already been
expecting for years. *What if it is one of my parents?* Yet that still didn't seem
right.

Then I looked over at my snoozing husband and thought, *No, Lord, please do not let it be Greg!* At that time, my biggest fear was that without my husband alive and holding me accountable, I would return to looking for love in all the wrong places. Then my mind wandered down the hall to my beautiful angel of a daughter and to my newborn son sleeping soundly through the storm in his crib. With tears streaming down my face, I begged the Lord, *Please! Do not let it be someone in this house!* A deafening clap of thunder boomed, and a brilliant bolt of lightning illuminated my bedroom, as if God were saying, *Yes, someone in this house is about to die.*

Drowning in my tears, I mentally wrestled with God for over two hours. None of my begging seemed to change anything, and I became emotionally drained from panic.

Then the Holy Spirit gently reminded me of God's promise that He would never give me anything I could not handle. I remembered how He had walked with me with such tenderness and compassion through the car accident years earlier. Once I embraced the idea that God would give me whatever strength I needed to endure yet another tragic loss, the storm abruptly stopped. No thunder. No lightning. No rain. Just silence. The first sound I heard was the beautiful melody of a chirping bird. I lay there for quite a while longer, thinking that birds never come out and start chirping immediately after a storm. When I still could not go back to sleep, I got up and ate a bowl of cereal. A full tummy eventually helped me return to my slumber.

The next morning, I told Greg every detail of the night's experiences. I asked, "Do you think I was dreaming?"

He turned the question back to me and said, "Do you think you were dreaming?"

I went to the kitchen and saw my empty cereal bowl and spoon in the sink. "No," I replied with worry, "I certainly wasn't."

THE LONGEST TWO MONTHS OF MY LIFE

Convinced that someone I loved was about to die, I would not let Greg leave for work each morning without a major production of hugs and kisses. I wanted to make sure that if he died that day, he would die knowing I loved him. I was hesitant to let either of my children out of my sight. I thought that as long as they were in view, I could keep anything tragic from happening to them.

This nerve-wracking scenario went on for almost two months. I was beginning to crack. Then on February 13, 1996, I went to my Bible Study Fellowship meeting, but that night I couldn't sit with my friends. I slid into the back pew alone, with tears of distress staining my cheeks. Silently but desperately, I cried out to God, *I cannot take this limbo any longer! Whoever it is in my house that has to die, so be it! But I can't stand not knowing anymore! Go ahead and do what You have to do!*

As the teaching leader began her lecture, she had us open our Bibles to John 12:24, "I tell you the truth, unless a kernel of wheat falls to the ground and dies, it remains only a single seed. But if it dies, it produces many seeds" (NIV).

I could not have heard God more clearly if He had appeared before me in person. It was me that had to die! I had to die to myself.

Although I heard what God said, I left the meeting not really understanding what He meant. Angrily, I yelled at Him underneath my breath all the way through the parking lot, "What part of myself have I not died to, God? I wanted to be a doctor, but You wanted me to be a youth minister, so I gave You my vocation! I wanted to spend more money decorating the house, but You asked us to pledge more to our church, so I gave You my finances! I just gave You permission to take your pick of my husband or either one of my children! What more do You want from me? What else is there to die to? I don't know what kind of game You are playing, God, but if there is something that I still need to die to, You are going to have to show me very clearly because I haven't a clue!"

AN ANGEL IN A TANK TOP

The next day I had a noon appointment with a man who taught my aerobics class (I'll call him James). What prompted me to accept his lunch invitation was the suspicion that he did not know Jesus. So when he asked me to lunch, I thought this would be a good opportunity to tell him about a loving God who wanted a personal relationship with him.

However, as I was driving to meet him, my prayers were not only for James's soul but also for my focus to remain on the business at hand. His bulging biceps were a potential distraction from my mission. (Had James not been so attractive and had I not basked in the attention he lavished on me during aerobics class, I am certain I would not have been so concerned about his salvation.)

As we sat in the noisy cafe, I tried to work up the nerve to put my agenda out on the table and talk to him about God. James turned the tables by leaning over into my face and asking in a low voice, "Do you know why I invited you to lunch today?" Feeling extremely uncomfortable, I responded that I did not.

He whispered, "Because you have a neon sign on your forehead that says you are hungry for attention and affection!"

Fearing that I was being propositioned, I asked, "Well, I am a happily married woman in ministry, so how do I get that neon sign off my forehead?"

James grinned and sincerely responded, "Shannon, you have got to die to yourself!"

Was I on *Candid Camera*? Had this man been a fly on my wall over the past two months? Had he been reading my mail? Or had God sent him to confirm what He had told me the night before?

Attempting to gather my wits and hold back the tears that were quickly forming, I managed to ask, "How exactly do I die to myself? I really need to know!"

Just as Jesus spoke the truth in love to the Samaritan woman at the well in John 4, James held a spiritual mirror to my face that day. I often came to aerobics class not to sweat, but to make men sweat. Finally someone had the courage to help me see myself as too many others had already seen me, not as the pure bride of Christ, but as a walking target for inappropriate attention.

I couldn't deny that men rarely treated me with the respect I felt I deserved as a married woman in ministry. I had often wondered, *What is wrong with all these guys who flirt with a girl wearing a wedding ring on her finger? Why would so many men make passes at a woman driving a minivan with a Jesus bumper sticker and an infant seat in the back?*

Never before had it occurred to me that my mannerisms were often teaching men to treat me in such disrespectful ways. "I only dress like other women dress, walk like other girls walk, and talk like others talk," I had reasoned in the past. I had chimed in with many females who claimed "If a guy can't handle the way I look, that's *his* problem." This attitude was a problem—*my* problem!

Once all these things were brought into the light, I couldn't deny that I enjoyed being flirted with and the feeling of power it gave me. This knowledge brought enlightenment and demanded change. Was I going to hear the gentle rebuke that God was giving me? Would I respond with humility and repentance? Was I going to conduct myself as an attention-hungry flirt and a tease or as a pure and spotless bride? I imagine that Jesus was awaiting my response with bated breath.

My husband had obviously been awaiting my response to these questions as well. I shared my revelations with Greg later that night after having lunch with James. When he heard the details of the conversation, tears of relief flowed down his cheeks as he explained, "Shannon, I've been praying for five years that someone would come along and help you understand these things about yourself. I have never had the words, but I have known that the Lord would send an angel into your life to reveal these things to you."

We agreed that I should see a female Christian counselor, and I began my journey toward sexual and emotional restoration. Through this experience, I was finally able to turn off the neon sign on my forehead and let God remove the "scarlet letter" from my sweater. As I grew confident that God had truly clothed me in white, I began to live that way.[1]

This story is a vivid illustration of (1) how God goes to great lengths to call our attention to the sin that separates us from Him, and (2) how He longs for us to respond when we sense His loving correction. When He puts His finger on an area of our lives that needs remedying, will we ignore Him and continue to live to satisfy our selfish desires? Or will we humbly die to ourselves and receive His correction so that we can enjoy unbroken intimacy with Him? If your choice is the latter, let's look at how we can do each of these things.

DYING TO OURSELVES OVER AND OVER AGAIN

After I had completed six months of intense individual and group counseling, my therapist kicked me out of her office saying, "Go! You are healed! You don't need me anymore." I was feeling great about all that I had overcome and how much I had grown and matured through the process. However, it didn't take long before I realized that this dying-to-self thing wasn't a one-time shot. I had mistakenly assumed that I had arrived at a rock-solid place of commitment to a pure lifestyle, never to waver or budge.

After all, once you are dead, you can't get any more dead, right? But this initial dying-to-self experience was only the beginning. My living sacrifice kept crawling off the altar as selfishness, anger, and pride continued to rear their ugly heads. If I was going to continue to put on my robe of righteousness, I had to learn to die to myself on a daily basis. I frequently meditated on the following scripture for the spiritual strength to keep dying over and over as needed:

> If any of you wants to be my follower…you must put aside your selfish ambition, shoulder your cross, and follow me. If you try to keep your life for yourself, you will lose it. But if you give up your life for my sake and for the sake of the Good News, you will find true life. (Mark 8:34–35)

Do you want to live as the spotless bride of Christ? If so, consider the main thing that Jesus said is required—putting aside our selfish ambition and following Him. What might this look like? Whenever we are tempted to do anything that would pose a threat to our righteousness and bring disappointment to our Bridegroom's heart, we do whatever it takes to resist the temptation and remain pure.

During one of the many seasons in which God was teaching me other ways I needed to die to myself, I felt convicted that I should no longer have private telephone conversations with a particular married man who would call me frequently while my husband was at work. While it initially felt rude not to return this man's phone calls, I knew if I talked with him, the conversation would eventually turn flirtatious, as it most often did. We didn't have caller ID back then, so I had to let the answering machine screen all my calls. Every time the caller hung up without leaving a message, I figured it was probably him. At one point, I wanted to pick up the phone so badly, but a red Sharpie marker sitting on the counter caught my eye. I sensed God saying, *Remember how I willingly died for you, Shannon. Now willingly obey Me and die to yourself. Don't go play in the mud. Remain white and pure for Me. Put aside your selfish ambition. Follow Me. I'll lead you to a much more peaceful season of your life, if you'll let Me.*

So rather than pick up the phone, I picked up the Sharpie marker instead. I drew big red circles on the palms of my hands as a reminder that I've been crucified with Christ. I was determined to die to myself so that Christ could live more fully in and through me. As I turned to my Bible for affirmation instead of turning to this married man, I came across Paul's words to the Romans:

> Well then, should we keep on sinning so that God can show us more and more kindness and forgiveness? Of course not! Since we have died to sin, how can we continue to live in it? Or have you forgotten that when we became Christians and were baptized to become one with Christ Jesus, we died with him? For we died and were buried with Christ by baptism. And just as Christ was raised from the dead by the glorious power of the Father, now we also may live new lives.
>
> Since we have been united with him in his death, we will also be raised as he was. Our old sinful selves were crucified with Christ so that sin might lose its power in our lives. We are no longer slaves to sin. For when we died with Christ we were set free from the power of sin. And since we died with Christ, we know we will also share his new life. We are sure of this because Christ rose from the dead, and he will never die again. Death no longer has any power over him. He died once to defeat sin, and now he lives for the glory of God. So you should consider yourselves dead to sin and able to live for the glory of God through Christ Jesus. (Romans 6:1–11)

Every small act of obedience loosens sin's grip on us. We don't have to be slaves to our self-destructive desires. We can die to ourselves and follow

God's lead into victory and abundant life. As I've increasingly learned to do this, I've come to feel more and more like Christ's true bride.

> *And now, Israel, what does the LORD your God require of you? He requires you to fear him, to live according to his will, to love and worship him with all your heart and soul.*
> DEUTERONOMY 10:12

When the Lord asks you to put aside your selfish ambition, rest assured His loving eyes are upon you. If you receive His correction, you will ultimately experience a much greater sense of peace. Psalm 94:12 says, "Happy are those whom you discipline, LORD, and those whom you teach from your law." Also, Proverbs 3:11–12 says, "My child, don't ignore it when the LORD disciplines you, and don't be discouraged when he corrects you. For the LORD corrects those he loves, just as a father corrects a child in whom he delights."

If we are willing to die to ourselves, we will also be willing to submit to God's correction when we do something that hurts our relationship with Him.

SUBMITTING TO GOD'S LOVING CORRECTION

My son recently reminded me about the connection between discipline and love. At ten years old, high-energy Matthew has experienced his fair share of spankings. At one time my husband theorized that perhaps spankings simply didn't work with our son, and we decided to abandon the corrective measure all together. But then we noticed something. Matthew seemed to be acting out all the more just to get our attention. It was as if he were saying, "Hey! Aren't you going to spank me? Don't you love me anymore?"

I prayed about how to handle our son's need for discipline, and finally one day as he was misbehaving, I asked, "Matthew, do you *need* a spanking?"

I was floored when he responded, "Yeah, I think I do."

After I spanked him, with tears in his eyes he hugged me as if to say, "Thanks, Mom. I needed that." The rest of the evening, I noticed how different his whole attitude was. He was courteous at the dinner table. He was punctual about getting his homework done. He even helped his sister with her chores. He was a completely different kid.

> *Then Jesus said to the disciples, "If any of you wants to be my follower, you must put aside your selfish ambition, shoulder your cross, and follow me."*
>
> MATTHEW 16:24

As Greg and I tried to analyze what we'd done differently, we realized that we usually waited until our son had pushed us over the edge and then spanked him out of anger. The spanking provided a little venting for our own personal steam but didn't really do much for Matthew's behavior. But this time I had disciplined our son out of love, and it turned him into a loving little kid.

In contrast, when God disciplines us, He never does so out of anger. The Bible tells us numerous times that God is slow to anger and abounding in love (see Exodus 34:6; Numbers 14:18; Nehemiah 9:17; Psalms 86:15; 103:8; Joel 2:13; Jonah 4:2, NIV). When God disciplines us, it is truly because He wants the best for us. It is God's kindness that leads us to true repentance (see Romans 2:4). His compassionate correction should produce in us the same result as my correction produced in Matthew—we should soften and become loving as we submit.

If you have been disciplined often by God because of recurring sin in your life, remember the following encouraging examples from Scripture:

- Even though David committed adultery with Bathsheba and had her husband murdered, David submitted to God's correction and was still declared to be "a man after [God's] own heart" (1 Samuel 13:14). Regardless of your sin (past, present, or future), you are never disqualified from having a special place in God's heart.

- About the sinful woman who anointed Him, Jesus said, "Her sins—and they are many—have been forgiven, so she has shown me much love. But a person who is forgiven little shows only little love" (Luke 7:47). If you have been forgiven little, then you probably love little. But if you have been forgiven much, you more than likely love much. That's cause for celebration.

- To the church in Laodicea, the Lord said, "I am the one who corrects and disciplines everyone I love. Be diligent and turn from your indifference. Look! Here I stand at the door and knock. If you hear me calling and open the door, I will come in, and we will share a meal as friends. I will invite everyone who is victorious to sit with me on my throne, just as I was victorious and sat with my Father on his throne" (Revelation 3:19–21). The church that received the harshest rebuke and was infamous for being "lukewarm" was also promised a place at God's right hand. Regardless of how far we've fallen, if we respond to God's loving correction, we will be invited to sit with God on His throne. We can't earn that place of prominence on our own, but God grants it to us freely.

When our spirit is broken over the chasm between God's perfection and our imperfection, we please God. Psalm 51:17 reminds us, "The sacrifices of God are a broken spirit; a broken and contrite heart, O God, you will not despise" (NIV). Indeed, a broken and contrite heart is exactly the response God longs to receive from us. Only then are our hearts in the correct posture to receive from God all of the love, comfort, and direction that He longs to give His bride.

ENJOYING UNBROKEN FELLOWSHIP

What bride wants to feel distanced from her groom? One of the most compelling factors that should motivate us to die to ourselves and submit to God's correction is that sin causes us to be spiritually and emotionally separated from our Bridegroom.

A similar dynamic often takes place between me and my kids. Because I love them, I discipline them when they are not behaving as the godly young man or woman they truly are. I can tell if they are genuinely repentant by the way they relate to me as I am correcting them. If their hearts are hard toward me, they have their arms folded and find it difficult to look me in the eye as I speak to them. But if they realize what they've done is wrong and are truly sorry for it, they'll look directly into my eyes when I am talking to them, because they want assurance that I forgive and love them. That's how we are with God. Our hardened, sinful hearts cause us to want to run and hide from Him, just as Adam and Eve did in the Garden of Eden. But our soft, repentant hearts long to restore our close connection with God and receive assurance that things are still good between us.

When we sense God's displeasure and desire for our repentance and restoration, it's a sure sign of His love for us. If you feel His correction, rejoice that you are deeply loved by your Creator, and enjoy unbroken fellowship with Him by responding with a humble, repentant heart. However, if you are in sin, but do not feel conviction from God about it, you may need to ask yourself, *Have I somehow managed to kill my conscience? Have I alienated myself from God such that I am failing to hear His loving call to repentance?*

Because God so deeply desires unbroken fellowship with us, He loves us right where we are, regardless of how entrenched in sin we've become. However, He loves us far too much to just leave us there. While He has paid our bride price and provided us with a white wedding gown, He desires for us to live the way He sees us. He wants us to embrace our role as His bride, for that is ultimately where we will find peace and fulfillment.

PUTTING PRINCIPLES INTO PRACTICE

Of course, dying to ourselves, submitting to God's correction, and communing more intimately with Him as a result is a process that can occur either quickly or slowly based on the response we choose.

For example, when I was in elementary school, I had a bad case of sticky fingers. I often roamed the downtown stores after school until my mother got off work at 5 p.m. Mom would give me a little spending money, but my shopping trips often turned into shoplifting trips once my money ran out. God prompted me throughout those years to do the right thing and confess what I had done, but I ignored His gentle rebuke.

Then in my early thirties, years after I had stolen for the last time, I realized I was at a spiritual impasse with God, as if He wouldn't give me further direction until I had obeyed His previous prompting to humble myself, return to those stores, and repay what I had stolen. I made a list of five stores, along with the approximate value of the merchandise I had stolen from each of them. I asked Greg if I could take enough money out of our checking account to reimburse them, and then I faced each store manager one by one. None of them could believe what I was doing, but they were all very gracious in accepting my apology and my remuneration, and each extended the forgiveness that I sought. One woman even said with tears in her eyes, "If only every person listened to God like that! Bless you for your honesty." Of course, if I were all that honest, I'd never have stolen in the first place or waited so long to correct the situation!

Even after I had made things right in all those stores, my conscience still wasn't completely clear, nor did I experience the spiritual breakthrough that I longed for in my relationship with God. There was one more thing I had stolen as a child—my grandmother's necklace—and it had bothered me for more than two decades. I was only ten when I stole it and then lost it, and I had no idea that it was a special gift to her from my grandfather. Although the episode came to light almost immediately, and I had apologized to my grandmother back then, I had never actually repaid her for the loss. Prompted by the Holy Spirit, I wrote her a letter, telling her how grieved I was that I had ever stolen the necklace, and I sent her a monetary gift with my sincere hopes that she would accept it. To my surprise, her response was that she didn't even remember my stealing a necklace from her. I assured her that I had and begged her to accept my act of restitution. My grandmother's response told me that she never held it against me, although I had held it against myself all along.

A few weeks later, my grandmother died suddenly. My aunt called to say she had taken the money and purchased a cross necklace for my grandmother to be buried in. I was completely at peace with that. When I think of how I would have felt at my grandmother's funeral had I not obeyed the Holy Spirit and written that letter, I cringe. It seems as if God was preparing me for her death by giving me the gifts of a clean conscience and a healed relationship. I just wish it hadn't taken me so long to respond to my guilty conscious and find peace. I lost far too many years worrying that she thought less of me for stealing her necklace, when in fact, she hadn't even thought of it for decades.

No matter what we have done, God is determined to reveal the fault lines running deep within our character so that we will allow Him to strengthen those faults and restore our relationship with Him. Our fault lines are the most vulnerable points that Satan will continue to target. He uses our favorite flavors of sin to attract us into taking a detour off the path of righteousness and to distract us from living the life we truly desire to live.

Several times since my sticky-finger days, I've been faced with the temptation to steal without really stealing. Perhaps a store clerk accidentally gave me too much change, or a cashier put something in my bag without ringing it up on her register, or maybe my child walked out of a store, holding an item that he or she assumed I had paid for when, in fact, I hadn't. I'm happy to say that each time something like this has happened, I've promptly called the store's attention to it and offered to make restitution, usually to their pleasant surprise. Why didn't I just take the mistakes as a bonus and walk away? Because it would be a sin, and I know that sin displeases my Bridegroom and separates me from Him. The guilty conscience that results would ultimately drive me to confess and make restitution anyway, so why not walk away with my head held high rather than cast down in shame for not doing what I know to be right? The integrity and dignity that I feel when I do the right thing is far more valuable than the $20 excess change or the $10 pot roast I could have walked away with in my bag.

Of course, stealing, flirting, dressing immodestly, and many of the other sins that have been stumbling blocks to me may not pose much temptation for you. You may have other flavors of sin that you've developed an appetite for. Regardless of the nature of our selfish desires, we must still consider how we will respond to God's correction.

A NO-BRAINER DECISION

If you'll listen with your heart, you'll hear Jesus calling, *Will you die to yourself so that I can live in you and through you?* How will you respond? Will you live in a mud puddle of sin and selfishness? Or will you allow God to pull you out, cleanse you completely, and clothe you in white for your wedding day?

For the woman who loves Jesus without limits, these questions may seem like a no-brainer. Logically, it just makes sense for us to say yes! to all that our Bridegroom is offering us. However, sometimes we forget we are the bride of Christ, and we fail to live accordingly. But don't worry. His grace is sufficient (see 2 Corinthians 12:9, NIV). Even when we forget, Jesus will always remember who we are and whose we are, and He is happy to give us a gentle reminder when we need one.

Of course, He doesn't need to write a note on the palm of His hand to remember that you are His bride. He takes one look at His palm and sees the nail scars that purchased your redemption. He's forever aware of your righteousness, for it was His blood that purchased that irrevocable gift for you. Receive it. Cherish it. Celebrate it. And know that you look stunning in white!

5

Forsaking All Others

When a bride commits her life to her groom, she promises to "love, honor, cherish, and obey…for better or worse, for richer or poorer, in sickness and in health, until death do us part." There is nothing conditional in these words. A bride does not vow to love only when her groom is lovable, to honor only when he is honorable, to cherish as long as there's something in it for her, to obey as long as she trusts his judgment, or to remain committed as long as it's easy. She commits to love her groom wholeheartedly. She commits to being completely his.

God wants us to do the same in our relationship with Him. He wants us to love Him with a reckless abandon kind of love. A love that says, "I'm going to love You no matter what it takes, no matter where it takes me, even if the going gets tough or times get hard. I'm going to love You. Period. And that will never change."

In *Every Woman's Battle*, I describe an incredibly vivid dream I had several years ago as a result of asking God to show me what women need to understand about His heart for them. In my dream, a bride is milling around the room, soaking up the praises and adoration of her wedding guests. However, her groom is nowhere to be found. As I scan the room, he finally comes into my view. He's standing in a corner, looking down at the wedding ring his bride has just placed on his finger. Yet, he is shedding tears of sadness because she doesn't feel the need to have him by her side. She isn't introducing him to her friends, and he appears to feel shunned. As his tears fall onto his hands, I notice the nail scars and realize the groom is Jesus.

I awoke from my dream with a sick feeling in my stomach. "Lord, is this how I made You feel when I was looking for love in all the wrong places?" I wept at the thought of hurting Him so deeply.[1] As I have become more aware of the pain I cause my beloved Bridegroom when I fail to cling to Him, I've become more motivated to forsake all others.

Are you ready to do the same? Are you ready to cleave only to Him, regardless of where that takes you? If so, let's look at some of the things we need to leave behind if we want to find genuine fulfillment and learn to love Jesus without limits.

FORSAKING FALSE FULFILLMENT

Some of us look to food or substances in an effort to fill a void, numb a pain, or satisfy something deep within ourselves. Perhaps one more drink will relax us, or a certain pill will take the edge off our anxiety, or another slice of turtle cheesecake will make us feel better. These things may indeed provide temporary relief or satisfaction, but they eventually do us more harm than good. We can only find lasting relaxation, peace, and contentment through an intimate relationship with the Lover of our souls.

If food or substance abuse hasn't been a temptation for you, perhaps you've searched online, in the pages of a romance novel, or between the sheets for your soul's satisfaction. Before you turn off the computer, you need just one more ego stroke from the stranger you've been interacting with in cyberspace...before you put down the book, you have to read just one more chapter to see if the heroine finally submits to the passions that rage within her for the suave and debonair hero of the story...before you go home, you must have one more dance at the club, just to see where things might lead with this handsome sweet talker. While human relationships (virtual, fantasized, or real) seem to ease our emotional pain and provide some relief from loneliness, no one can ease our pain and loneliness the way God can.

Perhaps you've looked to more socially acceptable forms of satisfaction, such as the pursuit of higher education, or corporate ladder climbing, or trying to be a perfect wife and Super Mom. You keep thinking, *If I just complete one more degree or certification, if I receive a few more promotions, if I can get a few more kudos out of my husband or kids—then I'll know that I am really something special.* But no matter how hard you look to any of these things for your ultimate satisfaction, they all fall short in the end. Why? Because we simply can't find our heart's true delight anywhere else except in the presence of Jesus.

In the words of Women of Faith dramatist Nicole Johnson, "We are like Swiss cheese, and the holes in us are actually supposed to be there. The holes are the things that make us who we are. The holes are the places God has reserved in us for Himself! The longings identify our real hunger. A hunger that drives us to Him to be satisfied."[2]

FORSAKING ALL PRESENCE IMPOSTERS

At this point some of you are likely thinking, *But, Shannon, I've never looked to anything but God to satisfy me. I read my Bible frequently, and I am active in my church and trying to live a pure life. But for all my efforts, God still seems far away. I don't seem to have the kind of close relationship with Him that you describe. What's up with that?*

I've come to learn that the things of God do not necessarily equate to God Himself. Service and Bible study do not always translate into intimate time spent with Him. In our humanness, we are perfectly capable of doing good works and studying our Bibles completely separate from the Lord. Sometimes we think we are experiencing God Himself, when what we've done is settled for an imposter.

Are there things—even good things—you do for God in place of pursuing His presence as a person? What things make you think you are experiencing God, when you are really just doing things *for* God? Perhaps you, like me, have found service and study to be tempting substitutes for true intimacy with God.

I fell into this trap in my early days of youth ministry. I had the Jesus posters on my office walls and an entire wardrobe of T-shirts with Scripture slogans. I spent every Sunday and Wednesday leading a youth group, and most days in between preparing for yet another topical lesson, Bible study, or mission project. I spent hours counseling teens and their parents and led summer camps every year where many came to know Christ or recommit their lives to Him. But I've come to recognize that God was not working *through me* as much as He was working *in spite of me*.

What was my problem? My motives. Rather than seeking intimacy with Him, I was meeting with God only to get a handout of something I could use in my ministry. I was trying to impress other people and convince myself that I was really a good person. I thought if I could outweigh the unrighteous acts in my life with enough righteous acts, then I'd be acceptable to God and others and feel better about myself. My goal wasn't a selfless one of serving my Lord, but a selfish one of serving my own self-esteem. My spirituality was a false persona, a mask I hid behind so others would think I was holier than I really was.

Scripture mentions our motives and intentions in many places, particularly in the following verses:

> People judge by outward appearance, but the LORD looks at a person's thoughts and intentions. (1 Samuel 16:7)

People may be pure in their own eyes, but the LORD examines their motives. (Proverbs 16:2)

When the Lord comes, he will bring our deepest secrets to light and will reveal our private motives. And then God will give to everyone whatever praise is due. (1 Corinthians 4:5)

We can tap dance our way through this world, but God sees the "why" behind our tap dance. As creative and inspiring as my youth-ministry efforts may have been, much of it was done out of selfish ambition, a desire to further my own kingdom. I liked that the kids thought I was cool. I enjoyed having the respect and appreciation of their parents. I relished being thought of by my pastor as an asset to our church. It seemed on the surface to be all about God, but deep down, most days it was really all about me.

Of course, at the time I didn't realize I was operating out of selfish ambition. I thought I was living my life for God. But if that were the case, why didn't I have a more intimate relationship with Him? Why wasn't I inspired to spend time basking in His presence, simply enjoying His company? Why wasn't I seeking His plans for my youth group rather than relying on my own creative ideas? Why was I only taking my Bible off the shelf when I needed to prepare a Sunday-school lesson or write a newsletter? In hindsight I can see that I was preaching something (having a "personal relationship" with Christ) that I wasn't experiencing myself. I was relying on my own efforts, and it was exhausting. In fact, it was less than two years before I resigned, because I felt I had nothing more to give.

I believe many other Christians are also on the verge of burnout for the same reason. Their relationship with God is not intimate. In their attempt to find fulfillment, many study and serve God more and more yet spend less and less time simply enjoying the presence of their Bridegroom. Consequently, their strength often wanes.

Joanna Weaver gives an insightful diagnosis for such situations:

> We can get caught in [a] performance trap, feeling as though we
> must prove our love for God by doing great things for him. So
> we…implement great ministries and wonderful projects, all in an
> effort to spread the good news…. While the world applauds
> achievement, God desires companionship. The world clamors,
> "Do more! Be all that you can be!" But our Father whispers, "Be
> still and know that I am God." He isn't looking as much for work-
> ers as he is looking for sons and daughters—a people to pour his
> life into….
>
> Frustrated and weary, we can nearly break under the pressure
> of service, for there is always something that needs to be done.[3]

None of us can make any lasting difference in our own strength,
regardless of how strong we may be. When service takes the place of an
intimate relationship with God, we'll always burn out long before the
work is done.

But service and study aren't the only presence imposters. We can also
mistake people, places, and things for God's presence. For example, you
might think that simply because you attend church, you've spent time
with God. Not so. Many pews are warmed from Sunday to Sunday by
folks just going through the motions and playing church. Or perhaps you
think that frequent theological discussions with your pastor or Sunday-
school teacher constitute a personal encounter with God. But we don't
need an intermediary to help us experience God. In fact, a dependence on
a more spiritually mature middleman is an inadequate substitute for a personal, passionate pursuit of knowing God ourselves. Even time spent reading great books about God cannot take the place of our own interactions
with God Himself.

This truth was brought home to me the other day when I was talking with a dear friend about how much joy our special relationship brings me. We talk often, calling or e-mailing each other several times throughout the day whenever something spurs our thoughts in the other's direction. We think very highly of each other, and it comforts me that another human being is so interested in sharing my life and in sharing her life with me. While I was expressing my feelings to her on one of our walks, I also had the thought that many people could claim to know me because they've read some very intimate details of my life in books I've written. But to know me through a book can't compare with how my friend knows me so personally and so intimately.

Suddenly I sensed God saying, *Uh-huh! That's exactly how I feel, Shannon. Lots of people know many things about Me because they've read My Book, but they have yet to experience the joy of being in an intimate friendship with Me.*

Think about it. Would you enter a room where your closest friend was waiting, sit down near her, pick up a book about her life and read a chapter or two, then stand up and leave without personally interacting with her? Of course not. So why are we tempted to do that with God?

We often fail to comprehend that He isn't just some distant Being responsible for our salvation. He's a real person with real feelings and real longings. He went to the trouble of creating us and redeeming us so He could enjoy an intimate relationship with us—forever.

If we long to be completely His, we must cling only to Him and forsake all presence imposters. We must also be sure that we aren't pursuing God in order to gain power or success.

FORSAKING IMPURE MOTIVES

None of us can deny that our almighty God possesses an enormous amount of power—infinitely more than we could imagine—and that He can provide us with incredible success in our endeavors. However, is our pursuit of God based primarily on these benefits? Do we get so distracted by the gifts that we fail to bask in our relationship with the Giver Himself? Do we see God merely as a means of possessing power and success?

Such could have been said for several characters in the Bible, particularly Simon the sorcerer. He claimed to be someone great and was very influential because of the magic he performed. The Samaritan people even referred to him as "the Great One—the Power of God" (see Acts 8:9–11). When Philip preached in Samaria, Simon followed him, amazed at the great miracles and signs Philip performed. Simon even became a believer and was baptized. As he witnessed people receiving the Holy Spirit when the apostles placed their hands on the people's heads, he desired to have such power as well and offensively offered money to the apostles in an attempt to buy it.

> "Let me have this power, too," he exclaimed, "so that when I lay
> my hands on people, they will receive the Holy Spirit!"
>
> But Peter replied, "May your money perish with you for
> thinking God's gift can be bought! You can have no part in this,
> for your heart is not right before God. Turn from your wickedness
> and pray to the Lord. Perhaps he will forgive your evil thoughts,
> for I can see that you are full of bitterness and held captive by sin."
>
> "Pray to the Lord for me," Simon exclaimed, "that these terrible
> things won't happen to me!" (Acts 8:19–24)

Simon was saying to Philip, "I'm not so sure the Lord would answer my prayer for protection, so you stand in the gap for me!" Simon didn't have the assurance of God's unconditional love and mercy because he didn't fully understand God's character and nature. He was more focused on getting something of value from God than on knowing God Himself. He was more concerned with the power to perform great acts than with allowing God to reign in his repentant heart.

Another character whose words revealed the selfish desires of her heart was Zebedee's wife. I can just envision this overprotective mom grabbing the arms of her sons, James in one hand and John in the other, then approaching Jesus with her presumptuous question, "In your Kingdom, will you let my two sons sit in places of honor next to you, one at your right and the other at your left?" (Matthew 20:21). She was concerned with status and power, but she was ignorant of the great price that Jesus must pay in order to assume His position of eternal King. Were they willing to pay such a price as well? Were they willing to suffer as Christ had to suffer?

James and John were confident that they were indeed willing, and Jesus agreed with them somewhat as He prophetically declared that they would, in fact, drink from the cup of suffering (Acts 12:2 tells us that James was the first apostle to be martyred, and Revelation 1:9 reveals that John suffered exile). However, Christ explained that the places of honor at His right and left hands could only be awarded by His Father. The other disciples were outraged that James and John would even pose such a question, revealing their own jealous desires for power as well.

All of this bickering about rank, privilege, and power sets the stage for Jesus' words of wisdom about what true leadership means.

> You know that in this world kings are tyrants, and officials lord it over the people beneath them. But among you it should be quite different. Whoever wants to be a leader among you must be your servant, and whoever wants to be first must become your slave. For even I, the Son of Man, came here not to be served but to serve others, and to give my life as a ransom for many. (Matthew 20:25–28)

Jesus' words cast a brand-spanking-new vision of leadership in the minds of the disciples and in our minds as well. We receive true power when we humble rather than exalt ourselves. We are successful in leadership when we give our lives away in service to others.

Paul knew the secret to achieving power and success. "It is not that we think we can do anything of lasting value by ourselves. Our only power and success come from God. He is the one who has enabled us to represent his new covenant" (2 Corinthians 3:5–6).

> *My goal is God Himself, not joy nor peace,*
> *Nor even blessing, but Himself, my God.*
> —OSWALD CHAMBERS, *My Utmost for His Highest*

Indeed, the pursuit of power and success for their own sake is futile. It is the person of Jesus Christ who gives us the power to do things that will have eternal significance. Apart from a personal relationship with Him, we are just spinning our spiritual wheels.

If you are reading this book, you likely long for a deeper relationship with God. I want you to know that God longs for intimacy with you even more. Based on His constant pursuit of us, I think it's safe to say His is the greater longing. Ours is the greater need (for where would we be without Him?), but He has proven by His death on a cross that His is the greater desire.

When we respond to this desire and relate to God in such a personal way, we discover the intimate connection we long for. Then we can bask in a bridal love for Christ rather than settling for a "bridle love."

BRIDLE LOVE VERSUS BRIDAL LOVE

If you are a country girl like me, you are well aware of what a bridle is. It's an instrument that you harness over a horse's head. For what purpose? So you can lead the horse exactly where you want him to take you. Unfortunately, many Christians only develop a bridle love for Christ—we follow Him because we want Him to take us exactly where we want to go—toward power and success on this earth and toward heaven once it's our time to leave. But He longs for our bridal love instead.

Many people in the Bible thought they had a bridal love for God. They knew Him and believed they were serving Him wholeheartedly. But in Matthew 7:21–23, He says to these folks, "Not everyone who says to me, 'Lord, Lord,' will enter the kingdom of heaven, but only he who does the will of my Father who is in heaven. Many will say to me on that day, 'Lord, Lord, did we not prophesy in your name, and in your name drive out demons and perform many miracles?' Then I will tell them plainly, 'I never knew you. Away from me, you evildoers!' " (NIV).

In his book *A Heart Ablaze,* John Bevere offers great insight as to why Jesus would say such a thing:

> You may question, "If Jesus said He had never known them, how could they cast out devils and do miracles in His name?" The answer is that these men and women join themselves with Jesus for the benefits of salvation. Though they accept Him in order to be saved, as with the children of Israel, they do not come to know the heart of God; they go only as far as His provision. They seek Him for their own benefit; their service is self-motivated, not love-motivated.
>
> In Jesus' statement "I never knew you," the English word *knew* is the Greek word *ginosko.* In the New Testament it is used to describe intercourse between a man and a woman (Matthew 1:25); it represents intimacy. Jesus is actually saying, "I never intimately knew you." Moses intimately knew God, but Israel knew Him only by the miracles He did in their lives. This is no different.
>
> We read in 1 Corinthians 8:3 (NKJV), "But if anyone loves

God, this one is known by Him." The word *known* is the same Greek word *ginosko*. God intimately knows those who love Him.[4]

Are you encouraged by this, or are you worried by the knowledge that you can't pull any wool over God's eyes when it comes to whether you love Him or simply love the things He does for you?

GETTING REAL WITH GOD

In light of the fact that God knows you so much better than you know yourself, ask Him to reveal your motives to you. Consider asking Him, "What people, places, or things do I substitute for You, Lord? What are the things I need to forsake in order to embrace You as my soul's ultimate satisfaction? What activities do I engage in that are really just imposters of Your presence? What do I need to forsake in order to be completely Yours?"

If you are willing to forsake all others and cleave only unto Him, you'll come to truly know God. Not just godly people, places, or things, but God *as a person*. As you do, you will likely fall more deeply in love with Him, and you'll want to find meaningful ways to express your love, which is the subject of our next chapter.

Becoming Fluent in the Language of Love

G reg was out of town, and I had sent our children to their grandma's so I could fast and pray about a new season of ministry I felt we were about to enter. Late in the day, my hunger pangs reminded me just how little I enjoy fasting. Determined to pray through them, I opened my Bible and came upon Matthew 9:14–15, "One day the disciples of John the Baptist came to Jesus and asked him, 'Why do we and the Pharisees fast, but your disciples don't fast?' Jesus responded, 'Should the wedding guests mourn while celebrating with the groom? Someday he will be taken from them, and then they will fast.'"

I looked in a New Testament commentary for further explanation of this passage and read, "Bridegroom's attendants fasting while the feast is in progress! How absurd, says Jesus as it were. Disciples of the Lord mourning while their Master is performing works of mercy and while words of life and beauty are dropping from his lips, how utterly incongruous!"[1] It occurred to me that Jesus was saying, "Now is not the time to fast, Shannon. I am with you! This should be a time of celebration!" but I wanted to make sure it wasn't just my extreme hunger talking, so I asked for further confirmation from His Word. I soon came across verses such as "Taste and see that the LORD is good" (Psalm 34:8) and "Look! Here I stand at the door and knock. If you hear me calling and open the door, I will come in, and we will share a meal as friends" (Revelation 3:20–22). That last scripture cinched it for me. I knew God was inviting me to dine with Him. To feast in His presence rather than fast.

I went to the kitchen to see what I could find to eat that would be appropriate for such an occasion. Peanut butter and jelly or canned ravioli would never do, so I reached into the freezer and came up with a petite filet mignon, broccoli and cheese sauce, and Sara Lee strawberry cheesecake. As I prepared my feast, I sensed God saying, "Set the table for four. There will be four of us dining tonight. We're all coming, so let's make it a dinner party!" So I set a place for each person—God the Father, Jesus the Son, the Holy Spirit, and myself. I created a warm, festive mood with fine china and silver, linen napkins, fragrant candles, and soft music in the background.

Of course I enjoyed the food, but I enjoyed the conversation most of all. For almost two hours, I expressed my love and thanks for specific ways the triune God had helped our family in the past. I asked questions about this new season of ministry we were about to enter into, and I listened as He spoke to my heart with words of encouragement. While some would think me crazy to pretend to have dinner with imaginary guests, I know it was much more than that. It was a private feast with intimate friends. And it was wonderful. I felt so very honored and overwhelmed that I had been invited to dine with such distinguished guests.

If you have read any of my other books, you know that my relationship with God hasn't always been this intimate and satisfying. Many times throughout previous years I sat at dinner tables across from various men while starving for any attention and affection they might toss my direction. But no dinner invitation has thrilled me the way this invitation did. Recognizing that the Creator of the universe wanted to have an intimate dinner with *me* caused every fiber in my being to want to respond with a resounding *Yes!* It inspired within me a deep passion and a desire to express the depth of my love.

THE LANGUAGE OF LOVE

When we know that God loves us completely and unconditionally, we can't help but offer Him our utmost praise and adoration—to offer Him our worship, which is the language of our love. God alone is worthy of our worship, which is defined by Webster as "to regard with great, even extravagant respect, honor, or devotion."

When a bridal love for Christ wells up in our hearts, we find ourselves singing not only about Him but also directly to Him, for we know He is listening with delight. We sing Him our praises, not just on Sundays, but every day of the week. I even find myself waking up many mornings with a worship song already in my mind. And we don't just read someone else's words as a prayer to God. We speak to Him out of the depths of our own emotions and experiences. We cry out to Him in times of pain, despair, and confusion because we know we can be honest with Him about our struggles. We verbalize our petitions to Him because we have confidence that He hears us and that He cares about the things we care about. We craft sweet sentiments that relay to Him just how awesome and wonderful we think He is.

When we worship God in this way, we are saying, "I want You to have control over my life because Your ways are higher than my ways...Your thoughts are higher than my thoughts...Your love is greater than my love. Teach me Your ways, Your thoughts, and Your love so that I can be more like You, Lord!"

THE REASON FOR WORSHIP

We owe God our love and most sincere worship simply because of who He is and because He works so diligently to capture our hearts and attentions. *Yes, God is working diligently to capture your heart and attention.* Allow that thought to draw you into His presence the next time you feel as if God has His back turned toward you in disdain for neglecting your quiet times. That's simply never His stance. He always has His face toward us and His arms open wide, eager for yet another intimate encounter... and another...and another. He is always eager to receive our worship. He is always eager to reveal Himself to us more fully. God doesn't play hide-and-seek. He says to you now, just as He said through Jeremiah long ago, "You will seek me and find me when you seek me with all your heart" (29:13, NIV). He longs to be found and adored by His creation. Claim this truth. Worship Him.

In his book *Cure for the Common Life*, Max Lucado eloquently explains why we should wholeheartedly offer our extravagant worship to God.

Worship.... The word conjures up many thoughts, not all of which are positive. Outdated songs. Cliché-cluttered prayers. Irrelevant sermons. Odd rituals.... Why worship?...

Honest worship lifts eyes off self and sets them on God.... Worship gives God honor, offers him standing ovations.... Worship places God on center stage and us in proper posture.... Worship adjusts us, lowering the chin of the haughty, straightening the back of the burdened.... We worship God because we need to.

But our need runs a turtle-paced distant second to the thoroughbred reason for worship.

The chief reason for applauding God? He deserves it. If singing did nothing but weary your voice, if giving only emptied your wallet—if worship did nothing for you—it would still be right to do. God warrants our worship.

How else do you respond to a Being of blazing, blistering, unadulterated, unending holiness? No mark. Nor freckle. Not a bad thought, bad day, or bad decision. Ever! What do you do with such holiness if not adore it?[2]

Indeed, the true bride of Christ longs to adore Him. She looks for opportunities to steal away and express her tender affections to Him. She fuels her longings for her Lover each time she pours her heart out before Him and asks Him to draw her nearer to His precious side. She sets her eyes in His direction throughout the day, wondering when He will make His triumphant return for her. She knows no greater satisfaction than to simply and joyfully meditate on His name, Jesus. She carries a wonderful secret in her heart, a secret that stirs her soul and awakens her passions like nothing else: she is not just anybody. She has been chosen. Chosen to be His beloved bride.

Of course, our expressions of love are not limited to the songs we sing or the words we pray. We can also express our adoration of God through our actions.

Loving Him Through Our Actions

God views all our acts of worship as incredibly valuable and honoring. Every act of service done with a happy heart is worship of our Master. I've met many women throughout my years of ministry who worship God through their acts of service, some in high-profile positions, but most in strategic behind-the-scenes roles. Let me introduce you to a few of them.

- Ruth teaches second grade at a Christian school as an act of worship. With lesson plans, teaching, and grading papers, the hours are long, the pay is miniscule, and the stress is often high. But her six- and seven-year-old students are learning not just how to write in cursive, but also how to live with character.
- Cindi is helping her husband launch a new church, and she homeschools her four children as an act of worship. She's in constant motion and barely manages to steal a few moments to herself in the wee hours of the morning before everyone else rises.

But she's joyfully pouring strong foundations in people's lives for God to build upon.

- Kim is a single mom who worships God by using her people skills and sales experience to solicit sizable corporate donations to keep a global nonprofit ministry afloat. Thousands of people in third-world countries depend on her to procure the goods they need in order to survive.

What keeps all these women going? Their deep love for Christ and their desire to be His helpmates. These daily activities all serve as evidence of what these women know to be true—Jesus is worthy of their every act of worship.

You probably know many women who are equally as passionate about their calling to serve God with their gifts and talents. We all have special things we can offer Him as acts of worship.

Sometimes the best way we can express our love for our Bridegroom is by doing what He is asking us to do, even if it is momentarily stressful or seemingly impossible. Our obedience will ultimately bring us more joy and delight than we could possibly imagine. And I'm inclined to think that Esther and Mary would agree with me.

LOVING HIM THROUGH OUR OBEDIENCE

Even though God isn't specifically mentioned in the Old Testament book of Esther, Esther's story beautifully illustrates the profound impact and influence we can have on others when we express our love for God through our obedience. As a young virgin, Esther is recruited into King Xerxes' harem and eventually chosen from among all the other candidates to be his queen. However, trouble begins to brew in the palace when Esther's cousin, Mordecai, explains that the wicked Haman is plotting to have all the Jews killed. Something must be done to save God's people, and Mordecai knows that Esther may be the only one in a position to stop Haman's plot. Why should Esther care? Although the king doesn't know this, Esther is Jewish. It is *her* people who are in danger.

Mordecai lovingly challenges Esther, "Don't think for a moment that you will escape there in the palace when all other Jews are killed. If you keep quiet at a time like this, deliverance for the Jews will arise from some other place, but you and your relatives will die. What's more, who can say but that you have been elevated to the palace for just such a time as this?" (Esther 4:13–14).

Although approaching the king without an invitation could result in immediate death, Esther realizes that she may be God's chosen instrument to deliver the Jews from destruction. She responds to Mordecai, "Go and

The presence of God is the concentration of the soul's attention on God, remembering that He is always present. My friend says that by dwelling in the presence of God he has established such a sweet communion with the Lord that His spirit abides, without much effort, in the restful peace of God. In this rest, he is filled with faith that equips him to handle anything that comes to him. This is what he calls the "actual presence" of God, which includes any and all kinds of communion a person who still dwells on the earth can possibly have with God in heaven. At times, he can live as if no one else existed on earth but himself and God. He lovingly speaks with God wherever he goes, asking Him for all he needs and rejoicing with Him in a thousand ways.

—BROTHER LAWRENCE,
The Practice of the Presence of God

gather together all the Jews of Susa and fast for me. Do not eat or drink for three days, night or day. My maids and I will do the same. And then, though it is against the law, I will go in to see the king. If I must die, I am willing to die" (4:16).

Of course, Esther doesn't die. She has earned such great favor with the king that he offers to give her anything she asks, up to half of the kingdom. Her request is that she and her people be spared from Haman's plot to have them all murdered. If there were a red badge of courage in biblical times, it would have been awarded to the brave Esther. She was willing to risk her very life to be used by God. Her love of her Lord and His people knew no limits.

As we look toward the New Testament, another young woman stands out as being one whose choices expressed her love for God—Mary, mother of Jesus.

Imagine this scenario (see Luke 1). Although you are betrothed to a respected man, you are currently an unwed teenager. An angel appears to you and says you are going to have a baby and that the baby will be the son of God. In reality, most likely you would wonder what your breakfast cereal had been laced with if such a thing happened to you. Your second thought would likely be, *But what will the neighbors think? I'll be pregnant before I'm married!* And of course, convincing your fiancé that you had not been unfaithful when your expanding tummy indicates otherwise would be quite a challenge. But Mary doesn't panic. She simply inquires of the angel, "But how can I have a baby? I am a virgin" (verse 34).

The angel replies, "The Holy Spirit will come upon you, and the power of the Most High will overshadow you. So the baby born to you will be holy, and he will be called the Son of God" (verse 35).

Mary's trust is astounding, as she simply responds, "I am the Lord's servant, and I am willing to accept whatever he wants. May everything you have said come true" (verse 38). Although an angel informed Joseph that the child Mary was carrying was indeed from God, not everyone got that memo. I imagine the rumor mill ground out much gossip over the matter. Mary must have endured many sneers and scoffs, all for the sake of serving her Lord.

As I ponder Esther's amazing courage and Mary's confident trust, I imagine that their worshipful responses must have deeply delighted God's heart. As I think of their devotion, I ask myself, *Am I living out the same courage and trust? Am I expressing my love for my Bridegroom with my obedience? Am I loving Jesus without limits?*

Let's look at one more way we can express our love.

LOVING HIM BY BASKING IN HIS PRESENCE

While mountaintop experiences like the one I describe at the beginning of this chapter aren't an everyday occurrence, I intentionally pursue the presence of God every day, several times a day. Because I love Him, I want to be with Him, whether I'm doing something as sacred as singing a hymn or as secular as slicing a sandwich.

For example, as I get up and shower, I often thank God for clean, hot water, as I've been to many countries that don't have such a luxury. As I drive my kids to school, we pray out loud for God's protection and blessings for the day. On my way back home, I either sing songs to Him or imagine Him sitting in the passenger's seat, listening as I pour my heart out to Him. Or I just listen, asking Him to speak His words of wisdom to me. As I walk to the mailbox, I invite Him to walk and talk with me. As I sit down to write, I ask that His words flow through my fingertips. As I pull my goose-down comforter over my shoulders at night, I envision His loving hands tucking me in and His gentle kiss goodnight. I imagine Him whispering in my ear, *This was a good day*, or *We'll have a better day tomorrow.* Even if my ears cannot hear Him and my eyes cannot see Him, my heart and mind are attuned to His voice and His presence, and I know He is always near.

While God wants us to practice His presence in little everyday moments, He also longs to experience extended, uninterrupted time with us. I'd like to share some practical tips for experiencing regular intimate times with the Lord, but before I do, I want to stress that our relationship with God is just that—*a relationship*. It's not a set of rules, so don't get legalistic about these things, but merely use them as ways to enhance your fellowship time with God and to create a more appropriate setting to experience genuine intimacy with Him.

SEVEN SECRETS TO BASKING IN GOD'S PRESENCE

1. Remember that all love affairs are carried on *in private*. If the only time two people ever spent together was in a public setting, they wouldn't have a very intimate relationship, would they? The same is true with us and God. We can spend time with Him publicly at church or our Bible-study group, but it's really in our private moments alone with Him that we can be truly uninhibited and experience the much deeper level of intimacy that we long for. And Matthew 6:6 says, "But when you pray, go away by yourself, shut the door behind you, and pray to your Father secretly. Then your Father, who knows all secrets, will reward you." Therefore, seek to get away from everyone and everything that would serve as a distraction.

2. Establish a certain place where you will have regular devotional times with the Lord. Whether it's the living room, backyard, or your closet floor, make it your special place to rendezvous with Jesus. As you inevitably wrestle with the "Am I going to have a devotional time today?" question, envision Jesus sitting in that

regular spot, awaiting your arrival. Remember, He gets just as much out of your time together as you do, so don't keep Him waiting there too long before you join Him in sweet fellowship.

3. Establish a certain time that you can carve out of your day and write it into your calendar just as you would an appointment. Some people say that mornings are the best time for devotions, but I say do whatever works for you. Whether that time is before everyone gets up, after everyone has gone to bed, or on your lunch hour in the stairwell, it doesn't matter. It may vary from day to day based on your schedule. God doesn't require you to punch a time clock at a certain hour of the day. He just wants to spend as much time with you as possible.

4. A few things you might want to keep nearby are a Bible, devotional book, a journal and pen, sticky notes (for jotting down scriptures you want to post somewhere and memorize), a fragrant candle and matches, a CD player and worship CDs, and pictures of people you want to remember to pray for.

5. You might also find that using a timer is beneficial. I started out using a timer saying, "I'm going to spend at least one hour with God" as a way of making me remain focused longer. But I've found that time flies by so quickly and I get so lost in His presence that I actually need the timer to keep me from going too long and making everyone late getting out the door in the morning.

6. Write your prayers in the form of love letters to God in a journal. As you read over things you wrote long ago, they can serve as spiritual markers of where you've been and where God has led you. On occasion, spend your time thumbing through the pages and praising God for His faithfulness.

7. Remember that conversing with God isn't a one-way conversation. Eight times in Revelation the churches are instructed to listen and "hear what the Spirit says" (NIV). He communicates clearly, but we must listen with our hearts rather than our ears. Allow plenty of time to just sit and listen to what God may be saying to you, keeping in mind His loving nature. Also, when you write in your journal, write letters to yourself from God as well, penning the words you sense Him saying to you. Compare those words with what He says in the Bible to make sure you are hearing Him correctly, as He never contradicts Himself.

As you try to establish a regular routine of basking in God's presence, keep in mind that it's easier to act your way into a new way of feeling than to feel your way into a new way of acting. Oftentimes I don't feel God's presence, but as I choose to enter into it as best I know how, my feelings eventually catch up. I may not sense the earth tremble every single time I commune with Him, but our love for one another is a fact, not a feeling. We must spend time alone with Him simply because we need it, and because He longs for time with us as well.

These times of close connection aren't an option for we who long to be completely His. They are our very life and breath. It becomes something we yearn for, something we crave, something we simply cannot and will not live without.

Jesus' yearning for this kind of quality time with us is evident in His final words to His disciples the night before He gave up His life for us:

Remain in me, and I will *remain* in you. For a branch cannot produce fruit if it is severed from the vine, and you cannot be fruitful apart from me.

Yes, I am the vine; you are the branches. Those who *remain* in me, and I in them, will produce much fruit. For apart from me you can do nothing.... If you *stay joined* to me and my words *remain* in you, you may ask any request you like, and it will be granted! My true disciples produce much fruit. This brings great glory to my Father.

I have loved you even as the Father has loved me. *Remain* in my love. (John 15:4–9)

Notice Jesus doesn't give the disciples a pep talk about all He wants them to take care of while He is gone. He doesn't leave them with a honey-do list or a chore chart. He knows that abundant fruit will automatically result if they simply remain connected to Him. He passionately pleads with them as if to say, "Although we have to be apart physically, we can remain connected spiritually. Please, please, remain connected with Me! I love you, and I don't want you to try to live without Me!"

His intent today is the same as it was over two thousand years ago. His purpose is not that we will *accomplish more* for Him, but that we will be *more connected* to Him.

OUR GREATEST ANTICIPATION

God has already initiated a divine courtship with you. He has paid the bride price for you and clothed you in white. He has extended His extraordinary marriage proposal to you. As you respond to Him by forsaking all others and becoming fluent in the language of love, you'll begin to yearn for His return, just as is written in the closing chapter of Revelation:

The Spirit and the bride say, "Come." Let each one who hears them say, "Come." Let the thirsty ones come—anyone who wants to. Let them come and drink the water of life without charge....

He who is the faithful witness to all these things says, "Yes, I am coming soon!"

Amen! Come, Lord Jesus! (Revelation 22:17, 20)

When Jesus indeed returns, our deepest hope and God's greatest desire will at last be fulfilled. We will take our rightful place of honor next to our heavenly Bridegroom and be forever joined to Him as His spiritual bride.

7

The Ultimate Wedding Gifts

Believe it or not, one of the most treasured gifts I've ever received is one I actually had to pay for myself. One day when my son was in kindergarten, he was packing all his stuff into his backpack and suddenly realized he was forgetting something. "Oh, Mommy, can I have five dollars?" Matthew asked with his big brown eyes staring up at me expectantly. When I asked what he needed the money for, he responded, "I can't tell you 'cuz it's a secret." Since it was the last week of school before the Christmas holidays, I suspected what he was up to and couldn't deny his request.

When Christmas morning arrived several days later, Matthew placed a small, unwrapped box in my hand, along with two dollars worth of change from the five dollars he had borrowed. As my son eagerly awaited the expression on my face, I tucked the money into the pocket of my robe and proceeded to open the box. To my surprise and delight, I discovered a very large, plastic ruby-and-cubic-zirconia ring, one that actually looked similar to the ring my grandmother used to wear when I was a little girl, although Matthew would have never known that when he picked it out.

I knew his gift would probably turn my finger green, but I didn't care. The thought of my precious son shopping around at his school's Secret Santa Workshop and choosing this beautiful ring just for me thrilled my heart. I scooped him into my arms for a tight squeeze and a loud smack of a kiss on his chubby little cheek. It didn't matter that the ring was far from the best quality. It didn't matter that it only cost three dollars. It didn't even matter that it was *my* three dollars that paid for it. What mattered was the loving, thoughtful spirit in which the ring was given, as if to say, "I love you so much, Mommy!"

> *Being with God is at the heart and soul of Heaven.*
> *Every other heavenly pleasure will derive from*
> *and be secondary to his presence. God's greatest*
> *gift to us is, and always will be, himself.*
> —RANDY ALCORN, *Heaven*

While we may get a chuckle out of Matthew's innocence, aren't the gifts we give to God much like the gift my son gave to me? If we think about it, even the greatest gifts we could ever offer Him are actually gifts He gave us the provision for. Have you placed a nice-sized check in the offering plate at church lately? Whatever income you may have been tithing on, He put all that money into your hands Himself. It only makes sense that we offer a portion of it back to Him with a happy heart, doesn't it? Have you served on a special committee at church or in your community lately? Isn't God the one who gave you the time, the talent, and the heart to serve in the first place? Have you sung Him a song of praise lately? Did you thank Him for the voice with which you sang? The very air in your lungs? A mind sharp enough to remember the tune and the lyrics?

Everything in the universe belongs to God; there's not one single thing we can offer Him that He didn't give to us in the first place. Nothing. Zero. Zip. Zilch. Nada.

God's Lavish Gifts

When it comes to unique gift giving, God's got the market cornered. His very best gifts to us are so special and unique that we will never find them available on any Internet Web site no matter how long we surf. They are not to be found even in the most creative of Neiman Marcus Christmas catalogs. We couldn't even find them if we searched every booth of every flea market on the planet.

Although God's lavish gifts are far too numerous to list, three in particular stand out to me as the ultimate in wedding gifts from our loving Bridegroom: redemption for our past, resurrection power for today, and a heavenly home for our future.

Redemption for Our Past

When I first sensed that God wanted me to tell others about my past sexual mistakes, I was frightened to the core. *But what will they think of me, Lord?* I wondered.

He answered, *It doesn't matter. The only thing that matters is what they think of Me. How will they know what My long arm of mercy and love can do in a person's life if you won't tell them about the depth of the pit from which I rescued you?*

So I stiffened my upper lip, took off my mask, and shared my testimony at various retreats for youth and for women. I was relieved to discover that people didn't seem to think less of me, as I had expected. Granted, some probably did without my knowledge, but many responded with gratitude and enormous relief. After a presentation, I'd often get statements like these: "I thought I was the only woman struggling with this issue! Thank you for your vulnerability!" "You mean there is hope for me even after all I've done?" "I wish I had the courage to be so open and honest with others." What I had expected was judgment and rejection, but I received unconditional acceptance and appreciation beyond my wildest imaginations.

It took almost two decades of God's working in my life, but He has transformed me from a poster child for teen promiscuity to a woman with a passion for God and for the sexual purity He calls us to. My greatest fear twenty years ago would have been for others to know about my secret sexual sins. Today, my greatest fear is for people *not to know* about the change that God has brought about in my life. I want to instill in others a great hope that God can and will make the needed changes in our lives when we submit to His transformation process.

On November 2, 1999, I wrote the following to God in my journal:

> You have ignited a passion in me that can only be satisfied by leading other women to sexual wholeness through a more intimate relationship with you. *My greatest misery has now become my greatest ministry!*

Since I first began writing books about sexual integrity for women, I've received hundreds of e-mails from readers claiming that they, too, are committing themselves to the task of reaching out to other women in a similar manner. I can still hardly believe how God has redeemed the parts of my life for which I was once most ashamed. What an incredible gift!

Of course, this pattern isn't unique to my life. Many other women are using their dark pasts to brighten the future of others. Christina, who was once a self-proclaimed Wiccan witch, now spends many weekends in a section of Dallas called Deep Ellum, searching for people with telltale signs that they are into witchcraft so that she can tell them about Jesus' genuine miracle-working powers. Melissa, who was placed in juvenile detention at fifteen for drug abuse, now sponsors newcomers to her local Narcotics Anonymous group. Samantha, who experienced an unplanned pregnancy at twenty-one, is now a social worker at a maternity home, helping young girls screen potential adoptive parents for their unborn babies or coaching them in caring for their newborns if they choose to parent the children themselves. All of these women would echo my previous sentiment. Like me, their greatest misery has now become their greatest ministry.

Not only does our heavenly Bridegroom redeem our pasts, He also gives us power to overcome our struggles in the present.

Resurrection Power for Today

This world is jam-packed with temptations, tests, trials, and tribulations. Jesus said so Himself when He proclaimed, "In this world you will have trouble." However, He doesn't leave us there. In the same breath He also says, "But take heart! I have overcome the world" (John 16:33, NIV). In other words, the power that Jesus Christ provides to all who believe in Him is greater than the power the world has over us.

Clearly, Jesus doesn't promise to remove all our recurring troubles. But He has given us the power to survive them and even to thrive in spite of them. That's what being an overcomer is all about.

Jesus didn't leave us to face our troubles alone. He sent His Holy Spirit to be our personal, on-call 24/7, never-charge-you-a-dime, incredibly insightful Counselor. Through the Holy Spirit, we gain the necessary power to transcend our struggles and the strength to endure the temptations that this world throws our way.

Along with the gift of resurrection power, we also receive many other gifts, including greater understanding and peace of mind and heart. Jesus' words remind us of these gifts that God gives us through the Holy Spirit:

> But when the Father sends the Counselor as my representative—and by the Counselor I mean the Holy Spirit—he will teach you everything and will remind you of everything I myself have told you.

I am leaving you with a gift—peace of mind and heart. And
the peace I give isn't like the peace the world gives. So don't be
troubled or afraid. (John 14:26–27)

Paul's words to the people of Philippi also remind us that we can experience Jesus' resurrection power as we depend on Him:

I no longer count on my own goodness or my ability to obey God's
law, but I trust Christ to save me. For God's way of making us right
with himself depends on faith. As a result, I can really know Christ
and experience the mighty power that raised him from the dead. I can
learn what it means to suffer with him, sharing in his death, so that,
somehow, I can experience the resurrection from the dead!

I don't mean to say that I have already achieved these things or
that I have already reached perfection! But I keep working toward
that day when I will finally be all that Christ Jesus saved me for
and wants me to be. (Philippians 3:9–12)

A divine Counselor. Peace of mind and heart. The same power that
resurrected Jesus from the dead. These are not things that Santa or the
tooth fairy can deliver. Only the Holy Spirit can give us such extraordinary gifts. We can't buy them, even with the combined net worth of Bill
Gates, Oprah Winfrey, and Warren Buffett. God's gifts are priceless. And
believe it or not, they are sufficient to help you live in a way that demon-
strates the depth of your love and commitment to the Giver of those
gifts.

No temptation is too strong. No test is too difficult. No trial or tribu-
lation is too taxing. With the Holy Spirit as our guide, the peace of God
on our side, and Jesus' 24/7 resurrection power, we are more than con-
querors (see Romans 8:37, NIV). We are the pure and holy bride of Christ.

While we can't live perfect lives this side of heaven, we can be perfected (improved more and more) through the power that the Holy Spirit makes available to us.

But what about Satan's schemes to deafen us to the voice of the Holy Spirit, steal our peace, and rob us of our power? Granted, he has a plan to try to strip us of these wonderful gifts. But let me remind you of several truths about Satan.

He is not the evil counterpart to God. His power is limited. He has nowhere near the power to do evil that God has to do good. Satan's powers pale in comparison to our Lord's! You may say, "But Satan has a whole army of demons working against me!" But Satan's legion of demons is only one-third the size of God's legion of angels that protect you (see Daniel 8:10–11 and Revelation 12:4).

Satan is not omniscient as God is, so he does not know everything. He may see our actions, but he does not know our thoughts, for only God knows our hearts and thoughts. Satan is also not omnipresent, so he cannot be more than one place at a time. Given the size of the whole earth, he can't possibly waste too much of his time tormenting you. He's got bigger fish to fry.

And here's another newsflash: we humans have even been given powers that Satan doesn't have, such as the ability to multiply ourselves through childbirth. Satan can't do that. He still has the same number of demons as he's always had. His troops are no larger today than they've ever been. We often cower at the thought of the evil one, but we fail to recognize that God has already given us His resurrection power, which is more than sufficient to reclaim the authority that Satan once stole from humanity in the Garden of Eden.[1] So buck up, Cowgirl! "Greater is he that is in you" (the Holy Spirit) "than he that is in the world" (Satan) (1 John 4:4, KJV).

In addition to a redeemed past and resurrection power for today, God also gives us the gift of a heavenly home for tomorrow.

A Heavenly Home for Tomorrow

The longer I live, the more I appreciate the earth's majestic beauty and magnificent wonders. However, my heart still cries out for far more than this world has to offer. I can't help it. I'm a perfectionist, and I want perfect health and perfect relationships and a perfect home in a perfect environment. I think God must be somewhat of a perfectionist too, because He has fashioned such a perfect place for each of us who has accepted His extraordinary proposal to be His beloved bride.

Ecclesiastes 3:11 (NIV) puts my longing into words, as it says that God has "set eternity" in the human heart. We naturally long for something beyond what this world has to offer. We instinctively crave what only heaven can provide. Of course, we may not be aware that eternity is what we long for, because it's hard to imagine what eternity will be like. We mistakenly envision heaven as a celestial place where we will sit on clouds and play harps all day, every day, day in and day out, forever and ever and ever and… Ugh! How boring! Who can look forward to something like that?

Fortunately, the Bible tells us that eternity will be nothing like that at all. Pastor Randy Alcorn searched the Scriptures from Genesis to Revelation and wrote an incredibly insightful book (appropriately titled *Heaven*), which reveals much of what Scripture has to say about our heavenly home. According to Alcorn, the best way to envision heaven is to imagine the presence of all the things we love about this world and the absence of all the things we hate. Imagine all the wonders of nature, such as oceans and mountains, without any hurricanes or earthquakes or other natural disasters. Envision having a strong, fit body that never ages, never aches, never gets fat or flabby, never gets sick, and never dies. Imagine being around your family without anyone ever getting mad, getting even, or getting their feelings hurt. In heaven, everything is perfect. Heaven is sin free, guilt free, stress free, sickness free, and abuse free. Only peace and prosperity for all God's children to enjoy.

Not only that, but the fulfillment we experience from the things we enjoy will be exponentially multiplied. Food will taste richer. Friendships will be sweeter. Work will only bring fulfillment and satisfaction. Best of all, "We are looking forward to the new heavens and new earth he has promised, a world where *everyone is right with God*" (2 Peter 3:13).

As I have pondered heaven and begun to hunger and thirst for such a place, my burning question has been, "Will I get my own personal Jesus to fellowship with, or will I just be a face in the crowd of worshipers at His throne?" This question may sound a little silly or selfish, but I want to be a Jesus hog when I get to heaven. I don't want to wait in line to have Him all to myself. I don't want to need an appointment to get His undivided attention. I want to drink Him in all the time, anytime I want.

In my conversations with others, I've learned I'm not the only one who feels this way. If you have a similar concern, you'll be delighted to discover that, according to Alcorn, God's glorious presence will not be in just one centralized location in heaven, but will permeate every part of it. No matter where we go in heaven, we will experience the fullness of God, the manifestation of His presence, and unbridled fellowship with Him. Alcorn suggests, "God's glory will be the air we breathe, and we'll always breathe deeper to gain more of it. In [heaven], we'll never be able to travel far enough to leave God's presence. If we could, we'd never want to."[2] Can you imagine never feeling distant from God again? Never asking if He is there or if He hears your voice? Never wondering how He feels about you or what He would say to you? In heaven, you will experience God firsthand—His feelings and His thoughts will be made known to you as fully as He knows them Himself.

SHOWERED WITH GOD'S GOOD GIFTS

I remember the several bridal showers I was given just prior to our wedding. They were such a blessing and I felt so honored by everyone's good wishes and gifts. But I also remember how I got a little depressed after we had opened all the gifts and sent out all the thank-you notes. No more large gatherings of all my nearest and dearest friends. No more fun games. No more presents to unwrap or pictures to snap. Just memories. Sweet memories.

But the wedding gifts that God showers upon you and me will never have to be just memories. They are truly gifts that keep on giving and giving. We can continue to use the testimony of how God has redeemed our pasts as a way of glorifying Him and blessing others. We can claim His resurrection power to overcome the troubles that each day brings so we become more and more like Him. And when our lives are over, we'll spend eternity with our heavenly Bridegroom in the magnificent mansion He's built especially for us, where we will experience never-ending joy, dancing, and feasting. We will forever bask in the presence of the One whose love for us is perfect.

What a cause for celebration!

8

Mathematical Miracles

A third-grade girl brought home all As on her report card, with the exception of a D in math. Her mother insisted that if the girl couldn't bring that math grade up, she'd be removed from public school and enrolled in the parochial school at the Catholic church down the road.

The next semester arrived, and the girl brought home all As, except in math. In math, the highest grade she could muster was still a D. Remaining true to her word, the mother enrolled the girl in the parochial school and eagerly anticipated the next report card.

The day finally came when the daughter presented her grades—all As, including an A in math. "Hallelujah!" the mom declared, "But what have they done at the parochial school to help you do so much better in math?"

The daughter responded, "Mom, when I walked into that church and saw how they had nailed that man to the 'plus' sign, I knew they were serious about math!"[1]

While it may have been a childish error for this little girl to mistake a cross for a plus sign in this joke, such a description may be more accurate than one might think. Jesus describes Satan as a thief whose strategy is to steal, kill, and destroy, but then our Lord says, "My purpose is to give life in all its fullness" (John 10:10). In other words, Satan seeks to *subtract* and *divide* from our lives, but Christ seeks to *add* and *multiply*.

Over and over in both the Old and New Testaments, the Bible portrays God as one who adds and multiplies blessings into our lives:

- God told Abraham: "I will bless you richly. I will *multiply* your descendants into *countless millions,* like the stars of the sky and the sand on the seashore" (Genesis 22:17).
- He told Moses: "I will look favorably upon you and *multiply* your people and fulfill my covenant with you" (Leviticus 26:9).
- "And the LORD *multiplied* the people of Israel until they became too mighty for their enemies" (Psalm 105:24).
- "For through me your days will be many, and years will be *added* to your life" (Proverbs 9:11, NIV).
- "There will be joy and songs of thanksgiving, and I will *multiply* my people and make of them a great and honored nation" (Jeremiah 30:19).
- "But seek first His kingdom and His righteousness, and all these things will be *added* to you" (Matthew 6:33, NASB).
- "God's law was given so that all people could see how sinful they were. But as people sinned more and more, God's wonderful kindness *became more abundant*" (Romans 5:20).

Let's face it. Just like the third-grade girl who initially couldn't grasp math's complex concepts, we often fail to understand the exponentially abundant power of God's mathematical miracles. Perhaps we can learn some lessons from a particular widow and a young boy.

OFFERING WHAT WE HAVE

In the fourth chapter of 2 Kings, we find a woman facing an incredibly desperate situation. Not only has she just lost her husband in death, but her creditors are about to exercise their legal right to enslave her two sons as repayment for her outstanding debts. She approaches Elisha in faith that God will work a miracle through him. Elisha asks her what she has in the house, to which she responds that she has nothing at all except a single flask of olive oil. It's not much, but she offers what little she has.

Elisha responds, "Borrow as many empty jars as you can from your friends and neighbors. Then go into your house with your sons and shut the door behind you. Pour olive oil from your flask into the jars, setting the jars aside as they are filled" (2 Kings 4:3–4). The widow follows Elisha's instructions, filling every jar to the brim until there are no more jars left. As soon as every jar is filled to capacity, the oil stops flowing. She is able to sell the oil, pay off her debts, and take care of herself and two sons without further help from creditors.

I find it interesting that this mathematical miracle actually happened without the presence of Elisha in the room. It was just the widow, her sons, and God in the house, so there could be no doubt to whom credit was due. God took what the widow had to offer and multiplied it exponentially in order to demonstrate His power and provision. I also find it interesting that the flow of oil ceased when the woman ran out of empty jars. Indeed, the more of our own emptiness we present to God in faith, the more He is able to pour into us from His abundance!

Fast-forward almost one thousand years and you'll see God still up to the same mathematical mischief. A great crowd follows Jesus up into the hills because they had witnessed His healing miracles and perhaps sought one for themselves. Testing Philip, Jesus asks, "Where can we buy bread to feed all these people?" to which Philip replies, "It would take a small fortune to feed them!" (John 6:5–7).

Bzzzzzt! Wrong answer, Philip. Andrew then steals the spotlight, saying, "There's a young boy here with five barley loaves and two fish. But what good is that with this huge crowd?" (verse 9). Come on, guys! Don't you know who you are dealing with here yet?

Jesus instructs the disciples to have everyone—all five thousand men plus many more women and children—sit down in the grass. Then Jesus takes the boy's meager lunch in His hands, gives thanks to God, and passes out enough food to satisfy everyone's tummy as well as fill twelve baskets with some major leftovers! Par for the course, God proves that He can provide far more than we even need.

And how did the people respond to Jesus' mathematical miracle? They proclaimed, "Surely, he is the Prophet we have been expecting!" (verse 14), and they gave glory to God.

You may think these are great Bible stories from ancient times, but realize that God is still performing these kinds of mathematical miracles today. When we give what we have to Him, He blesses and multiplies our efforts. But if we withhold what we have, we may never personally witness His mathematical miracles.

Why is God willing to bless us with such abundance? Not to make us happy or comfortable, although these things often result. God performs mathematical miracles primarily to bring glory to Himself and to reveal His nature to us—to show us His overwhelming goodness and generosity.

Of course, God can multiply a lot more than just oil, bread, and fish. He can also multiply our time and resources—and even our money.

THE MULTIPLICATION OF MONEY

People tend to talk more about things that are extremely important to them than things that are not so important. Do you know what Jesus talked about more than any other subject? Money. One out of six of His statements recorded in the Gospels pertains to financial matters.[2] Jesus obviously knows how closely connected our hearts and our purses are, and apparently He wants to make sure our money doesn't come between Him and us.

Where our money goes says a lot about how we feel about God. In fact, we can determine what we value most by examining two things: our checkbook registers and our credit-card statements. What would yours say about your values?

Money is such a sticky subject that some pastors shy away from preaching about it too often for fear of angering their congregations. While many believers enjoy a good "name it and claim it" sermon, others will lambaste a minister for preaching what they consider to be nothing more than a "prosperity gospel." But if Jesus spoke so often of financial matters, shouldn't we?

> *If, for whatever reasons, we happen to be people of status, wealth, leadership, or influence, that doesn't mean that we are of greater value to the kingdom of God. It doesn't mean that we are better than other believers. It means that we are stewards of certain gifts, abilities, and opportunities. We are going to give an account to God for our use of those things. If God has given us money, wherewithal, personality, or whatever, when we take a step we influence others. Whatever the size of the sphere of influence, God calls us to lead in it.*
>
> — CHIP INGRAM, *Holy Ambition*

Having the proper mind-set about money makes all the difference in whether or not God will entrust mathematical miracles to us. If we want to love Jesus without limits, we will use our finances to do all we can for Him. In light of this, is it wrong to ask God to multiply our money or add to us financially so we might give more to Him? I think the answer lies with our motives. If our goal is greed, we've got trouble on the horizon.

But if our motive is to have more to give back to Him, I believe God is inclined to respond positively to those desires.

In Psalm 119:36, we see David begging God, "Do not inflict me with love for money!" Yet David was a very rich king who lived in a palace. Why did God bless him in spite of his desire not to be inflicted with love for money? Note that David never said, "Don't give me money." He said, "Don't give me a *love* for money." In other words, David didn't want to love money more than he loved God. David knew he couldn't serve two masters, "For you will hate one and love the other, or be devoted to one and despise the other. You cannot serve both God and money" (Matthew 6:24). I believe that because David was more concerned about loving God than loving money, God was able to entrust great riches to him. David declared where his love and loyalties lay when he wrote in Psalm 27:4:

> The one thing I ask of the LORD—
>   the thing I seek most—
> is to live in the house of the LORD all the days of my life,
>   delighting in the LORD's perfections
>   and meditating in his Temple.

David's loyalties were clearly with the God he loved; his was certainly a passionate bridal love.

In the spring of 2001, my husband and I came face to face with the question of where our love and loyalties lay. Through a series of events and as a result of much prayer, we sensed that God was calling Greg to leave his sixteen-year career at Baylor Hospital to serve in the finance department of Mercy Ships International, a mission organization comprised of floating hospital ships that provide surgeries free of charge to the world's poorest and neediest people.

The position they asked Greg to fill was at their land-based headquarters just down the road from our house, so it wasn't a question of our willingness to move to another part of the world to serve as missionaries. The question was whether we could afford to take such a leap of faith. Mercy Ships International is staffed almost entirely by self-supporting missionaries. Greg would be leaving his comfy position, high salary, full-benefits package, and 401k plan to work full time for an organization that could pay him nothing other than the satisfaction of knowing that he was where God had called him to be.

We would have to raise our own financial support, requiring large amounts of time meeting one-on-one with potential donors, sending out regular newsletters, speaking to church groups, and so on. We wondered if people would understand how vital Greg would be to the organization, since he wouldn't actually be on-board one of the ships on the front lines of the mission field. Would people be inspired to support a certified public accountant in Lindale, Texas, as opposed to the doctors or nurses on the ships in Honduras or Sierra Leone?

Greg and I both knew, without a doubt, that God was calling us in that direction. As we prayed and talked about what we should do, we agreed it all boiled down to one question: What did we love more? The security of a steady paycheck or the satisfaction of obedience to God? We didn't know how we would make ends meet, but we clung to this truth: *Wherever God guides, He also provides.*

So every month we asked God to multiply our meager funds so that we could afford to continue serving Him in this capacity. Although things were tight, our pantry always seemed to remain stocked, we always had nice clothes to wear, and our gas tanks never ran completely dry for lack of funds.

However, the stress was higher some months than others. One Christmas our van broke down and had to be put in the shop for a complete transmission overhaul. We didn't have the $2,000 required to get it out, so we had to forfeit any trips to visit relatives on Christmas Day. Nor did we have money to buy any Christmas presents, so we reluctantly paid for our gifts with our credit card. On Christmas Eve, I was staring out of my kitchen window, crying and praying, *Lord, surely You don't want us to sink ourselves deep in debt by living off of credit cards! Is it time for Greg to leave Mercy Ships and get a paying job again? Just show us what You want us to do and we'll do it.*

My prayer was interrupted when I saw a neighbor (whom we barely knew at the time) walking up our steps. I wiped away my tears, opened the door with a pasted-on smile, and stepped aside to allow our visitor in. He plopped a big turkey on my kitchen counter and said, "I can't stay, but I wanted to wish you all a Merry Christmas! And here's just an old card I had sitting around." I hugged his neck to thank him, and he quickly exited. A few minutes later I went to open the card and to my complete surprise found a check for exactly $2,500—enough to get the van out of the shop *and* pay for the Christmas gifts purchased on our credit card! It was an unbelievable gift from an unexpected source, but the best gift was the sense of awe we experienced that day. Surely God had orchestrated this miracle to remind us, "I know all your needs, and I'll continue providing for them, rest assured."

Our years of experience as fundraising missionaries have given us a new perspective on money. I believe the more we give to God and to others, the more He blesses us in so many different ways. *We simply can't out-give God, no matter how hard we try!*

The apostle Paul would agree, as he said:

Tell those rich in this world's wealth to quit being so full of themselves and so obsessed with money, which is here today and gone tomorrow. Tell them to go after God, *who piles on all the riches we could ever manage*—to do good, to be rich in helping others, to be extravagantly generous. (1 Timothy 6:17–18, MSG)

A good question to ask ourselves is, *Do I use my finances to help people, or do I use people to help my finances?* I believe that if we commit to using our money to help people, God is going to multiply our available funds. Why? Because it brings Him great glory to demonstrate His mathematical miracles through His people. Which people will He choose to demonstrate such miracles through? Those who love to give.

In his book *Making Jesus Lord,* Youth With A Mission (YWAM) founder Loren Cunningham tells of how God impressed it upon the organization to purchase an old abandoned hotel for the ministry's use in Kona, Hawaii. However, the property was entangled in bankruptcy proceedings, and the asking price was four times what they sensed God had told them to offer. Rather than operate in greed, as Cunningham had seen with the lawyers and bankers involved, he determined that the organization would move in the opposite direction of greed, giving generously even though they were in need themselves.

He writes:

> We had saved a large amount of money in our mission for the eventual purchase of a ship to carry practical aid and the Word of God to needy ports of the world. We had been praying and believing for that ship for a long time. But we decided God wanted us to give away the money—an amount in six figures to Operation Mobilization, another mission that was purchasing a ship for ministry.
>
> After we did this, a third Christian ministry, Daystar, gave us some property worth ten times more than the amount we had given to Operation Mobilization. That property gave us collateral to apply for a bank loan. We were on our way to buying a hotel!
>
> The days stretched into months as we continued the process of praying, giving, praising God for eventual victory, applying for bank loans and waiting to see if our bid would be accepted.

During this waiting period, the Lord showed us we were to have a time of generosity beyond cash offerings. We each asked God if there were something we owned that we should give to someone else. The purpose wasn't to get funds. It was simply an act of generosity to counter the spirit of greed operating in this situation.

For several days it continued, as individuals prayed, then went to their rooms and apartments and brought out their treasures. One family gave another a beautiful oil painting, others gave household items and favorite pieces of clothing. One boy gave away a surfboard for which he had saved for months, only to receive a pair of shoeskates from another kid. As we gave, it wasn't painful at all—it was fun! It felt like Christmas.

We saw the spirit of greed broken wide open in the spiritual realm in those months. Some may explain it away, saying we just got lucky. But all two hundred and fifty of us knew—it had been the simple act of giving that allowed us to finally purchase the property eleven months later at the exact price and terms which we had originally been given by the Lord—one-fourth the asking price of the owners.[3]

I can just imagine God's joy as He watched these missionaries giving so freely to other organizations and to one another, trusting wholeheartedly in God's provision rather than in their own abilities. I believe it gave God great delight to bless this team with a mathematical miracle.

Again, we simply can't outgive God! The more freely we give, the more freely He gives, and His storehouse is much bigger than ours. But, of course, finances aren't the only thing God delights in multiplying and adding to our lives.

He also takes great pleasure in…

The Multiplication of Our Influence

An even greater gift than increased finances with which to serve God is increased influence in people's lives. The more we can demonstrate God's love and faithfulness to others, the more receptive they will be to following Him. When you think of some of the most influential women of our time, you may think of Mother Teresa or Lady Diana. While these women did many things worth imitating, when I think of influential women, I think of Margaret Jean Jones.

In 1954, seventeen-year-old Margaret Jean became bedfast due to the progression of a disease that she had since the age of seven. Myositis ossificans progressiva (or Munchmeyer's disease) was an extremely rare illness that caused her muscles to stiffen like petrified wood. Too rigid to sit up in a wheelchair, Margaret Jean found herself marooned on a tiny bed-sized island in Cullman County, Alabama, with little hope of rescue. Eventually her jaw stiffened to the point that her food had to be blended to a smooth liquid in order for it to pass through her clenched teeth. The only area of her body with any movement at all was her right arm from her elbow to her fingers, which allowed her to nimbly maneuver a handheld mirror so she could look around the room and into visitors' faces.

Although movement was impossible, Margaret Jean still had feeling in her body, which made her pain unbearable at times. Tears often rolled down her cheeks, but she couldn't wipe them away. However, she says she found the strength not to fall into deep depression, sensing that God had *entrusted* her with this disease. She often thought of how Jesus had hung suspended on a cross—stretched out—unable to move His legs and arms, and she longed to make the most of her situation and serve Him in some way.

Margaret Jean's mother urged her to read and study, reminding her that even if she couldn't exercise her legs, she could at least exercise her brain. She had a love for reading and learning, and she found that talking with people (even through clenched teeth) fueled her natural curiosity. Relatives and family friends visited Margaret Jean often, sometimes bringing their own friends whom Margaret Jean had never met. She became acquainted with many interesting people and formed many meaningful friendships. She kept a guest book for a few years and found that she had more than five hundred visitors each year. Some of these visitors were retired people who reminisced about how their community used to be when they were young. These stories turned Margaret Jean into a local history buff, and an idea sparked in her imagination. She decided to write a book about the history of Cullman County.

This was quite the ambitious goal, considering Margaret Jean's condition and that there were no word processors in the early 1970s. Using a manual typewriter perched on a low tray above her stomach, Margaret Jean typed flat on her back with her one good hand, having to call her mother into her room every time she needed to have a mistake erased or a piece of paper removed. In time one history book turned into two award-winning books, and in 1979 she published her third, a personal memoir called *The World in My Mirror* in which she wrote:

> I became convinced that simply to idle the time away with no service to others or self-improvement was not only a fast and sure way of losing one's grip on reality, but also would be a dishonor to God....
>
> God is telling us not to waste physical, mental, and spiritual resources that he has entrusted to us. Whether they be many or few, humble or great, he appoints to us the responsibility of making the best possible use of them for his glory. And you can count on it, he does bless those efforts.[4]

Margaret Jean continued writing magazine articles and a weekly column for the local *Cullman Times* for over thirteen years, drawing many regular readers to her bedside just so they could meet her and thank her for the impact she had made on their lives.

For a season Margaret Jean also served as president of IDEAL Industries Inc., an organization whose goal was to promote *I*ndependence, *D*ignity, *E*mployment, *A*chievement, and *L*uster in the lives of the disabled. Through a federal grant in 1975, this organization opened a facility where many disabled citizens could receive meaningful training to help them live normal lives or ones with minimal supervision. The board of directors unanimously decided to name the center the Margaret Jean Jones Adult Activities Center.

Even after fifty years of being bedfast, Margaret Jean still has many visitors to her rural home in Cullman County—some who come to care for her since the passing of her parents many years ago, others who come strictly for the sweet fellowship. I was one of the latter recently. I remember my mother taking me to visit this extraordinary woman when I was a young girl. I recall admiring her tenacity and positive disposition even then. But visiting her again last spring as I was writing this book was a humbling and energizing spiritual sojourn for me. As I took a hot bath that night, I thanked God that I could care for myself, for I knew Margaret had not been able to bask in a tub for the past half century. As I took my children out to lunch and the park the next day, I realized what simple pleasures I take for granted. And as I tried to finish one more chapter, I realized just how easy it is for me to serve God with my portable laptop, two good hands, and full range of motion. How could I ever complain about my calling and turn these blessed opportunities into burdens?

As much as Margaret Jean has inspired thousands of people from her tiny bed-sized island to view life through a completely different lens, it's the Lord who has multiplied her influence exponentially. Even though she is unable to move, she is certainly a mover and a shaker for God!

Margaret Jean's life reminds us that we do not have to possess extraordinary gifts, talents, or abilities in order to be used mightily by our

Creator. We must simply remain connected to Him and be willing to let Him use all that we have to demonstrate all that He is. It is simply God's nature to bless—either in this lifetime or in the next—our honest efforts to glorify Him. Such attempts stand a good chance of being supernaturally and exponentially multiplied, for receiving glory is God's greatest desire, and giving glory to God is our greatest privilege.

Unfortunately, we can be tempted to fall into the trap of using God's gifts to glorify ourselves rather than Him. We will all be required to give account for our actions in heaven someday, not just for what we did, but for why we did it.

THE GREATEST DANGER OF INCREASED BLESSINGS

When God showers us with blessings, we can quickly forget who the money, talent, or credit really belongs to. Everything we own or possess is simply on loan to us from God to be used for His purposes, which is why we must be careful stewards of everything entrusted to us. We must vigilantly guard against the sin of pride.

In *It's Not About Me,* Max Lucado tells the story of a frog who developed a pride issue that eventually led to his demise. The frog's home was drying up, and if he didn't find water soon, he would dry up as well. He heard of an abundant stream on the other side of a hill where he could go and live, but his short legs wouldn't take him on such a long journey. So he came up with a clever solution:

> Convincing two birds to carry either end of a stick, he bit the center and held on as they flew. As they winged toward the new water, his jaws clamped tightly. It was quite a sight! Two birds, one stick, and a frog in the middle. Down below, a cow in a pasture saw them passing overhead. Impressed, he wondered aloud, "Now who came up with that idea?"

The frog overheard his question and couldn't resist a reply. "I diiiiiiiii…"

Lucado continues:

Don't make the same mistake. "Pride goes before destruction, and haughtiness before a fall" (Proverbs 16:18, NLT). Why are you good at what you do? For your comfort? For your retirement? For your self-esteem? No. Deem these as bonuses, not as the reason. Why are you good at what you do? For God's sake. Your success is not about what you do. It's all about him—his present and future glory.[5]

Let our response to every blessing be to offer it back to God, seeking ways to pass on His gifts to others so that we can be conduits through which His love, grace, and abundance flow.

GOD'S UNIMAGINABLE MATHEMATICAL RULE

Perhaps after reading this, you are thinking, *I don't have anything I can give God.* If so, I encourage you to consider how God does math problems.

When you and I memorized our multiplication tables, the easiest one to learn was zero, because zero times any other number always equals zero. Zero times one equals zero. Zero times ten equals zero. Zero times ten million still equals zero. But this mathematical rule has never applied to God.

Remember, God created the entire universe, billions and trillions of cells and molecules that form countless stars, planets, and galaxies. But what did He start out with on day one? Absolutely nothing. He made a vastly huge something out of absolutely nothing. How much was at God's disposal when He chose to fashion the first person through whom millions of other humans would eventually evolve? Nothing but some dust particles on the ground. He formed a living, breathing, working, playing, thinking, relating miracle named Adam, but He made him from scratch with no recipe to go by and absolutely nothing in the refrigerator or cupboard to start with.

So offer whatever you have to God, even if you think it isn't much. Then pray for a mathematical miracle, not so that you can have more, but so you can give more, help more, minister more, and bring all the more glory to your generous, heavenly Bridegroom.

Living an Irresistible Life

During a pivotal time in my life, I walked into a church desperately seeking the love of God, and thanks to Charlie and Martha Squibb, I found it. The first time I visited their church, I walked in on the arm of my boyfriend Ray. That may not strike you as odd, but I'm sure it struck Charlie and Martha as a little strange.

You see, I was twenty and barely out of mortuary college. Ray was forty and dean of that college. We made no bones about the fact that we lived just down the street—together. But Charlie and Martha didn't bat an eye at the twenty-year difference in age or our cohabitating status. They talked with us for quite a while and expressed their hope that we would visit their church again and get to know some of the other folks in the congregation. It was an inviting idea—not just to return to their church, but to get to know Charlie and Martha even better.

I continued visiting the church, but Ray preferred to stay at home, and we soon realized we couldn't continue in our dysfunctional relationship. Within a few weeks I moved out, gave control of my life back to God, and eventually met and married another man who attended that church—my husband, Greg. Had I felt judged at that church, I probably would never have returned. Charlie and Martha were so excited to come to our wedding, and they never said a condemning word to me about my previous living arrangement. They didn't have to. They just loved me into their congregation and prayed for me, and the Holy Spirit did the job that only He could do; He brought conviction and genuine repentance.

As the Beatles song says, "All you need is love…" Love *is* enough to draw us deeper into healing relationships with others and with God, and His love is enough to transform us into the people He desires us to be. Many of us prefer to reveal truth to others rather than simply show love, but truth is a sharp sword that can hurt rather than help others, particularly if love is absent. That's why we're told:

> Let love and faithfulness never leave you;
>> bind them around your neck,
>> write them on the tablet of your heart.
> Then you will win favor and a good name
>> in the sight of God *and man.* (Proverbs 3:3–4, NIV)

Notice this passage doesn't say to embrace self-righteousness, judgment, or condemnation, but rather to embrace love and faithfulness. Such character traits are what give us favor with people. Our goal shouldn't be as much to expose others' sins as it is to see people freed from their sin. How? By bringing them into a fuller awareness of God's perfect love, which completely covers our iniquities (see 1 Peter 4:8). We shouldn't just pity those experiencing spiritual, financial, emotional, or physical challenges—we should love them in their time of need.

How do we do this? Let some folks I've met show you.

- When Mary Ellen decided she was ready to leave her abusive pimp and her life of prostitution, she had nowhere to go except to a local church. With nothing but a suitcase full of seductive clothes and a look of fear and exhaustion in her eyes, she found refuge when Edith and Daniel invited her to stay in their guest room, free of charge. Ten months later, Mary Ellen had a respectable job that she enjoyed, a reliable car, her own apartment, and a much fuller realization of God's love, thanks to Edith and Daniel.

- Although Della lives on a very limited income as a retired senior citizen, she often cares for other people's children in her home during the day so she can earn a few dollars to send to missionaries she wants to support. We've been the recipients of Miss Della's generosity many times, and because of her loving heart, receiving twenty dollars from her is as precious as receiving two thousand from someone else.

- Beth has four young children of her own and all of the responsibilities that come with marriage and motherhood. However, Beth also made time to volunteer with the local CASA chapter (Court Appointed Special Advocates), serving as a liaison between abused children and the court to determine the best interests of the children. Her passion for abused and orphaned children blossomed to the point that she and her husband, Dave, completed all the paperwork, jumped through all the necessary legal hoops, and became foster parents to displaced children. Not only does Beth have plenty of love for her own family, but she has enough to go around to other children who may have never experienced God's love in their own dysfunctional homes.

- When I was growing up, we lived out in the country across the street from Mrs. Willaby, an elderly widow who didn't drive. One couple in the neighborhood drove her to church every Sunday morning and evening. Another neighbor took her shopping weekly. My mom planted a huge vegetable garden and shared freely with her as well. Mrs. Willaby may not have been able to get around town by herself, but because of the love of others, she never wanted for anything.

What do Charlie and Martha, Edith and Daniel, Della, Beth and Dave, and Mrs. Willaby's neighbors all have in common? They are living the kind of life that inspires us to greater heights. They are loving and caring for people. Their lives are an irresistible invitation for others to experience and demonstrate the love of God themselves.

AVOIDING A RESISTIBLE INVITATION

Sadly, too many well-meaning Christians attempt to evangelize others in very destructive ways. Rather than developing a deeper relationship, they focus on rules. Rather than exuding God's love, they exude legalism, creating an ugly, distorted picture of Christianity that no one would want to model. The Spanish Inquisition was an extreme example of this. Although we can't imagine anything like that happening in our day, people are still often offended and hurt by well-meaning Christians.

I met such a person a couple of years ago as we began working together on a project. When we met, she asked me, "Are you a Christian?" When I responded positively, she replied, "Well, I think you should know up front that I am not a Christian. I am Jewish. Does that bother you, or can you still work with me on this project?"

Taken aback by her candor, I said, "I can certainly work with you. However, I should give you the same opportunity. Are you comfortable working with someone who is a Christian?"

In the eighteen months we worked on the project together, this woman and I became good friends. Although we wanted to respect each other, neither of us felt that we had to hide our beliefs from the other. We were able to have several fantastic philosophical conversations. One day over lunch she said to me, "Shannon, I have to be honest. I've never met a Christian that I actually liked, but I've told all my Jewish friends about how you were considerate enough of my feelings to turn the tables and ask if I felt comfortable working with you."

I was shocked to learn that my question meant so much to her, but I was even more shocked to hear how poorly she had been treated by Christians in the past. She had endured tremendous rejection...prejudice...discrimination. She shared about her bitter memories of being asked to leave a private beach as a young teen because she was wearing a Star of David around her neck, and how she was never invited to stay overnight when her girlfriends had a slumber party. She found Christians had no love or tolerance for a Jewish girl.

When another friend of mine (who did grow up in a Christian home) became an adult, she decided she didn't want anything more to do with the whole church scene. When I asked her why, she responded, "I don't want to be like *those people!*" She went on to describe "those people" as judgmental gossips who walked around with their noses in the air and bragged about their faith. They spread rumors around the church about the misdeeds of others in town (all in the name of requesting prayer for that person, I'm sure) and saying things like "Christians shouldn't be doing things like that!" and "Tsk. Tsk. If they were real Christians..."

My friends weren't rejecting Christianity. They were rejecting gossip, judgment, legalism, prejudice, and discrimination, which we should all reject. Unfortunately, what nonbelievers often wonder about the Christians they encounter is, "Where is the love?" As the old hymn says, "They will know we are Christians by our love." But if they don't see love in us, they'll never see a true reflection of God in us either.

So many people will never read a Bible to discover God themselves. Instead, they read the believer. If someone were to read your life, what would they learn about God? about the Christian faith? Would they want to become like you? Would they want to get to know God better because of what they see in you? Would they feel judged and condemned, or would they feel unconditionally loved and accepted?

People won't listen to what we have to say about God's love for all humanity if our life doesn't line up with our lips. And since we can't give what we don't have, we must first extend the love of Christ to ourselves.

LOVING THE WOMAN IN THE MIRROR

Some would say that it is selfish to try to cultivate a deeper love for ourselves or that we already love ourselves too much and need to love ourselves less. But Jesus said that the first and greatest commandment is to "love the Lord your God with all your heart, all your soul, and all your mind," and that the second commandment, to "love your neighbor *as yourself,*" is equally important (Matthew 22:37–39).

> *Sociologists have a theory of the looking-glass self: you become what the most important person in your life (wife, father, boss, etc.) thinks you are. How would my life change if I truly believed the Bible's astounding words about God's love for me, if I looked in the mirror and saw what God sees?*
>
> —PHILIP YANCEY, *What's So Amazing About Grace?*

I want to pose the questions: How can we show others how much God's love changes a person for the better if others don't see us as the recipients of His lavish love? Does a woman who knows she is deeply loved by God consistently walk around moping, stressed, depressed, and complaining about life? Not if the love of God has entered her heart and penetrated her soul. I'm not saying that Christians should never feel stressed or depressed by life's difficulties, but we can't let our circumstances continually rob us of personally experiencing and expressing the love of God.

Indeed, what we believe about ourselves may seem like a small thing, but like the incredibly slight shifting of the earth's crust beneath the ocean floor, it is not. Those tiny shifts in the depths of the ocean cause a mighty chain reaction at the surface, possibly creating a tsunami of deadly force. Similarly, those little beliefs deep within your heart create an overwhelming effect on the surface of your life. Positive beliefs can create a tidal wave of blessings, while negative beliefs can create a tidal wave of destruction.

So what do you believe about yourself? Better yet, how do those beliefs line up with what the Bible says about you? In His Word, God declares that you are

- Christ's intimate friend (John 15:15)
- the Lord's chosen ambassador (2 Corinthians 5:20)
- God's trusted partner (2 Corinthians 6:1)
- the pure bride of Christ (2 Corinthians 11:2)
- an eternal citizen of heaven (Philippians 3:20)

Regardless of whether you recognize yourself in these passages or not, they express who you really are. You may not feel as if you are living up to this description just yet, but your Creator designed you with these purposes in mind, and Christ died to give you the authority to live out these roles with confidence.

We must make the connection between how we see ourselves and how we will approach life. If we see ourselves as bad, insignificant, inferior, or targets of God's wrath, we will never feel as if we can trust God to equip us, bless us, or use us. But if we see ourselves as the chosen bride of Christ, we will know beyond a shadow of a doubt that we can approach our Bridegroom with confidence and that He will give us all we need to do whatever He wants us to do (see Philippians 4:19).

For example:

- Rather than responding: "What, Lord? You want me to invite them to church? But they might get offended and think I'm self-righteous!"

The bride of Christ replies: "I'm not sure if they will accept the invitation, Lord, but that part is up to You. I'll gladly do my part out of my love for You."

- Instead of saying: "Me, volunteer one night a week at a homeless shelter? But Lord, I don't feel comfortable around the homeless. They make me nervous."

    The bride of Christ responds: "I may not feel comfortable, but, Lord, You love these people and have asked me to help care for them. I know You will be with me and teach me how to love them too."

- Rather than asking: "What's that, God? Go on a mission trip overseas? But I'd never be able to raise that kind of money!"

    The bride of Christ says with confidence: "I'm honored to wear Your name tag, Lord. Show me where to go and how to get there, and I'll pack my suitcase and passport."

When you sense God asking you to do something or talk to someone, remember who you are. You are not an abandoned orphan, but God's own cherished child whom He loves without measure. Whatever He calls you to do, He will lovingly provide the resources for you to be successful. Do you need strength? courage? a vision or a plan? finances? wisdom or discernment? Our God can provide all those things and more, in abundance. If we believe that His love is constantly flowing into us, that love will nourish us, equip us for our mission in life, and enable us to be sources of God's love in others' lives as well.

I can't stress enough that *how we see ourselves in relation to God has everything to do with our spiritual growth and effectiveness.* We must learn to see ourselves as His beloved bride in order to identify with the purpose for which we were created—to be in relationship with and in service to our heavenly Bridegroom.

As a reminder of God's love for me, on occasion I write myself a letter from God that includes the things I sense Him saying to me in that particular season. For example, on September 26, 2002, I wrote the following:

> I love you so much, not because of what you are (or aren't) doing, but because you are (and have always been) My beloved. I couldn't have loved you more even when you were sitting in that hotel parking lot or when you were lying in so-and-so's bed. My love for you has never been based on your performance or obedience. My love for you has been the same yesterday, today, and forever. The reason it feels so different to you in this season than ever before isn't because My love for you is any greater, but because *your* love for *Me* is so much greater. Because of this sacred romance purifying your heart and mind, you have also discovered a love for yourself and for others that is purely a gift from Me. You are highly favored not because of what you do or *who* you are, but because of *whose* you are and what I have already done for you. I have gone to the cross to make you Mine, Shannon. Indeed, you are irrevocably Mine, and I am yours for eternity.

Your Beloved Jesus

When God speaks to me like that, I feel wooed, pursued, and energized to go out and pursue others who are hungry to experience firsthand God's abiding acceptance and love. Let's embrace God's love for us so we can pour it out to others. Let's live loved.

Of course, it's one thing to offer God's unconditional love to our friends and family, but what about those who are seemingly unworthy of our love? If we are going to accurately reflect God's heart to the world, we will love even those who are incredibly difficult to love.

LOVING THE "HARD TO LOVE"

Perhaps you have heard the following verse:

> If your enemy is hungry, give him food to eat;
>   if he is thirsty, give him water to drink.
> In doing this, you will heap burning coals on his head,
>   and the Lord will reward you. (Proverbs 25:21–22, NIV)

This passage isn't saying we should do good in order to make our enemy feel bad or as an act of mean-spirited vengeance. Some theologians believe it may actually be a reference to an Egyptian ritual where a person would carry a basin of hot coals on his head as a sign that he had repented.[1] If so, heaping hot coals on your enemy's head would mean bringing that person's heart to repentance over his or her sin. Again, how do we do this? By loving that individual in spite of his or her sin and inspiring that person through our own lives to dive deeper into a love relationship with God.

Sometimes God calls us to love people in a way that will cost us a great deal. In his book *Making Jesus Lord*, Loren Cunningham writes about a pastor who had been imprisoned among hardened criminals for fourteen years, simply for preaching the gospel in the Soviet Union. Upon his incarceration, the pastor saw the prison as his mission field and sought a particular inmate whom he could focus his prayer and witnessing efforts toward. The man he chose was a vicious murderer with a reputation so fierce that even the prison guards were afraid of him.

Even though the pastor had to work twelve hours of hard labor each day, he chose to go without his meager ration of prison food in order to fast and pray for this murderer. In spite of his overwhelming need for rest, he chose to stay up and pray for this man's salvation rather than sink into the "comfort" of his bunk. Then God began to work a miracle. Cunningham writes:

One night while [the pastor] was on his knees praying and shedding tears, he sensed someone behind him. He turned.

The murderer was staring him in the face. "What are you doing, man?"

"I'm praying," he replied.

"What are you praying for?" he asked gruffly.

"I'm praying for you," the pastor answered, wiping away his tears.

Soon that man gave his heart to the Lord. The change in him was so drastic that news of what had happened spread through the prison. The head of the prison called the pastor in to ask what he had done to this man.

"I didn't do anything," he answered. "I just prayed for him. It was God who changed him."

The prison boss said, "There is no God. What did you do?"

The Christian repeated what he had said. "Well, I don't like this stuff about God," the prison official said, "but I like the changes I've seen. I'm going to give you a lighter job in the kitchen so you can have more time to do to others what you did to him."

This was known as the second worst prison in the entire Soviet Union, but after some time, more and more came to know Jesus and a real change took place in the overall atmosphere of the place.

The pastor was transferred to the worst prison in Russia, with the promise that if he could bring a change there, they would give him an early release.

A move of God started at the second prison, leading the pastor to write his wife a painful letter. He begged for her to understand his decision. He was turning down his parole in order to continue his ministry in that prison.[2]

The first time I read this story, it brought me to tears, and I have a difficult time not getting choked up every time I read it. It's unimaginable that someone could care so much about other people that he would give up his own life and freedom to reach them with the message of Christ's love. But oh how I long to have that kind of love myself for God and for others!

EXUDING A LOVE THAT EVERYONE CRAVES

As you love other people, your life will be an irresistible, living-and-breathing invitation for others to experience the love of God themselves. And when curious inquirers approach you, hoping to discover more about God's love, they will likely tell you things that they may not feel safe sharing with anyone else—sins that have served as barriers between them and God.

Keep in mind that you do not need to experience exactly what someone else has lived through in order to connect with that person. You can identify with far more people than you realize. Connecting with someone on a spiritual level is really a matter of identifying with the feelings that result from that person's experiences, then ministering to those emotions. You may not be a hardened criminal, but do you know what it feels like to be distant from God? You may not have grown up fatherless, but have you ever longed for attention and approval? You may not have ever been a prostitute, but have you ever experienced a sense of desperation and hopelessness? Maybe you've never been physically abused, but do you know what fear and anger feel like? Of course you do. Let us reduce our life's experiences to the common denominators of human emotion, and we'll realize that we are all far more alike than we are different.

Imagine what would happen if we learned to overlook our differences and focused instead on our similarities. Wouldn't we realize that we are all sinners in need of God's grace? Wouldn't we find it easier to love others with the love we've been given? Let's ask the Lord to help us pass the test of a true bride. Let's embrace His extravagant love, see ourselves as His beloved, and boldly entice others to experience His matchless love for themselves.

Of course, when we live such an irresistible life, we will eventually be approached by someone seeking to know more about this wonderful God of ours. They'll recognize that we are "walking the bridal walk," but are we "talking the bridal talk" as well? Would you know what to say to a potential bride in order to eloquently paint a vivid verbal picture of God's desire to become her heavenly Bridegroom? Could you effectively toss the bouquet to someone in order to invite her to the altar of God's love? In the next chapter we'll focus on crafting a testimony so that you can confidently share your own bridal story.

Tossing the Bouquet

O ne of my favorite parts of a wedding reception is the tossing of the bouquet, when all of the hopeful, yet-to-be married women eagerly gather around to catch the bride's flowers as she throws them over her shoulder and into the crowd. The sentiment behind this wedding tradition is that whoever catches the flowers is the next in line for her own wedding. Knowing firsthand the joy of finding a wonderful mate and becoming his wife, the bride is eager to wish another woman such happiness and fulfillment.

How eager are we to toss the bouquet to those who have yet to discover what a wonderful Bridegroom we have in Jesus? Do we know what we would say if we had an opportunity to talk with someone about our love for Him and His love for us? Do we truly have evangelism on our hearts and minds?

TELLING THE WORLD ABOUT GOD'S LOVE

When a woman marries, she becomes a partner to her husband. His goals become her goals. She longs to see his dreams fulfilled, and she does whatever she can to make those dreams a reality. This should also be true in our relationship with God. When we become Christ's bride, His agenda becomes our own.

Imagine being invited to a party where people know your name but have never seen your face. Unfortunately, you can't attend, but a friend approaches you and says, "Why don't you let me go for you? I'll wear your name tag, and everyone will assume that I am really you." Do you believe this person would represent you well? Would you trust her not to say or do anything that would discredit or embarrass you? Would you feel confident enough in her character to let her wear your name tag?

It's a scary thought. But do you realize that this is exactly the kind of trust God placed in us? As Christians, we go around wearing Christ's name tag. We represent Him to everyone we meet. Are we representing Him well? Are we focusing on the things that He would focus on in conversation?

Chances are, Christ wouldn't spend too much time chitchatting about the weather or what He saw on television last night. No, He would find a way to put His loving agenda out there on the table in conversations with those who have yet to experience Him personally. What is Christ's agenda? Consider the last words He spoke to His disciples before ascending to heaven. They are a commissioning for believers to express the love of God to everyone on the planet:

> Then Jesus came to them and said, "All authority in heaven and on earth has been given to me. Therefore go and make disciples of all nations, baptizing them in the name of the Father and of the Son and of the Holy Spirit, and teaching them to obey everything I have commanded you. And surely I am with you always, to the very end of the age." (Matthew 28:18–20, NIV)

> [Jesus] said to them, "Go into all the world and preach the good news to all creation. Whoever believes and is baptized will be saved, but whoever does not believe will be condemned." (Mark 16:15–16, NIV)

At Teen Mania Ministries, we teach that there are four distinct ways to fulfill this commission. We can (1) physically go ourselves, (2) financially support others who are called to go, (3) pray earnestly for those who go, and (4) encourage and mobilize others to go as our representatives.

While my family finds great joy in doing all these things, nothing is more fulfilling for us than going into other countries to deliver the message of God's great love. In 2001 all four members of our family acquired passports and laid them on the altar at our church, praying that God would give us opportunities to go wherever He would lead us and the courage to do whatever it takes to get there. Since then, we've traveled to Honduras, Costa Rica, Scotland, the United Kingdom, Sierra Leone, Germany, Holland, Panama, Romania, and Zimbabwe, either individually or as a family.

Keith Green, a Christian musician who was killed in a plane crash in 1982, was recorded on video at one of his final concerts as saying, "Nowhere on earth is the gospel as plentiful as it is here in the United States. You don't need a call—you've already had one. If you stay [in America] you better be able to say to God, 'You called me to stay home.' If you don't have a definite call to stay here, you are called."[1]

I couldn't agree more. Neither could Betsy and Jacob Smith. Three years after graduating from Oral Roberts University, and only days after purchasing a brand-new riding lawn mower, they felt challenged by Mark 10:21, where Jesus instructs the rich young ruler to sell everything and commit himself to the work of the ministry. After much prayer and confirmation, this couple decided to sell their mower, along with their house, furniture, cars, and even their pets. Why? So they could lighten their load enough to spend a year traveling through the most financially and spiritually destitute region of the world, the 10/40 window, in order to tell people of their Bridegroom's love.

The 10/40 window is a rectangular-shaped area extending from West

Africa to East Asia, from ten degrees north to forty degrees north of the equator. This region encompasses the majority of the world's Muslims, Hindus, and Buddhists. Ninety percent of the world's poorest people reside there. Even though 1.6 billion people within this area have never heard the gospel, only 8 percent of missionaries work in the 10/40 window. Betsy and Jacob spent one year connecting with people in twenty different countries including India, Mongolia, Niger, and Thailand, in order to produce a book and documentary that will inspire churches and other missionaries to concentrate their ministry efforts there (go to *www .acrossthe1040.com* for more information).

While not everyone is called to such a radical adventure, Betsy and Jacob's obedience to this calling vividly illustrates what it means to love Jesus without limits. They're giving God their all, and I have no doubt that God will reward their evangelistic efforts, both on this side of heaven and the next.

Of course, even if you feel called to stay in your own home country, you can still tell others about God's love for them.

TELLING OUR NEIGHBORS ABOUT HIS LOVE

I recently attended my twenty-year high school reunion where I offered and received many verbal testimonies about God's love and desire to be in relationship with us. Ramona Portley, whom I barely knew in high school and had not seen since graduation, came running toward me, gave me a big hug, and said, "Oh, Shannon, I have thought of you so often and prayed for you frequently over the years since your car wreck!" Most of my classmates don't even remember the accident, yet Ramona not only remembers, she has prayed for me many times since. Her sweet sentiments blessed me, and I felt a deep spiritual connection to her as a result. When I told Ramona that I was writing a book that would be dedicated to the woman killed and would tell of how God revealed Himself to me through her husband's merciful and loving response, Ramona committed to continue praying me through the process.

Other classmates were able to express their faith in various ways. An old friend showed me her family picture, saying, "I can't believe what a great husband and kids God blessed me with!" While sharing about his booming business, one man said, "I have to say that God has been so very good to us!" As a believer, I knew exactly what these classmates meant and was glad they knew whom to give credit for their healthy families and careers. If I had not been a believer, my curiosity would have been piqued over a God who blesses His people like that.

> *Wherever she goes, the bride of Jesus reflects something of heaven's radiance. A flame with love for her Bridegroom, she sparks off fires in the hearts of others. Such is the nature of the bride, for no one is a bride of Jesus who does not have a burning love and zeal for the kingdom of God.*
>
> —BASILEA SCHLINK, *My All for Him*

In fact, the wife of one of my classmates obviously had her curiosity piqued about spiritual matters. Over dinner, she asked me about the books I write. I gave her an overview of what the Every Woman series and Loving Jesus Without Limits series were all about. She responded, "I'd like to get a copy of the book for parents of preteen girls. It's funny, but it seems like every book I'm interested in lately just happens to be a Christian book even though I'm not a Christian. I've wondered if God is trying to tell me something."

Trying to hide my surprise and remain encouraging, I responded,

"Well, truth is truth, and it's hard not to recognize it and be drawn to it when you see it. I'll certainly give you a copy before we leave."

Later that evening, this woman saw me passing out books and approached me, asking for the copy I had promised her. As I handed a book to her, she grabbed my forearms and asked, "Would you pray for me?" Suddenly tears began streaming down her face, and she said, "I do think I hear God calling my name! I sense it and I can feel it!"

Hugging her tightly, I whispered into her ear, "If God is calling your name, girlfriend, don't resist. Go running to Him with reckless abandon! I have found such overwhelming joy and peace since I've let Jesus Christ be the lover of my soul. Don't miss all that He wants to offer you!" I told her that my e-mail address was in the back of the book and that I hoped she would feel free to ask questions and stay in touch. Now this woman is at the top of my prayer list—or my invitation list, as I call it.

MAKING AN INVITATION LIST

As you seek to toss the bouquet and tell your bridal story, who is your primary target? Is there a particular person or group of people whom your heart is inclined toward or who come to mind often as you pray? If so, I suggest you make a list of God's Most Wanted. Write the names of every individual you personally know is not yet a believer in Christ. Strategically place the list where you will be reminded to pray for those individuals often. As you pray, ask God if there is anything He would have you do or say to bring that person one step closer to a relationship with Him. Then if something comes to mind, be willing to do it.

In 1999 I was leading a group of women in a class on evangelism, and I asked them to write down the names of all those whom they knew to be nonbelievers. As we read the names aloud in prayer, I was surprised to hear that someone had written down the name Uncle Larry. I also have an

Uncle Larry, and although I had forgotten to write his name down, as far as I knew he was not saved.

So I committed to praying for my Uncle Larry every day that week. Come Saturday morning, I was hiding out on the floor of my closet, praying for my uncle for the fifth time that week. When someone knocked on the closet door, I was rather perturbed. I thought, *Can't a girl have some private prayer time around here?* Then Greg opened the door and stuck his head in, saying, "You have a visitor. It's your Uncle Larry!"

At first I freaked a little. I only saw my uncle once or twice a year, so for him to just show up out of the blue at the moment I was praying fervently for his salvation was almost too much to handle. But I pulled myself together, greeted him in the kitchen, then ushered him onto our balcony, where we sat chatting in the porch swing. He said, "Darlin', I don't know what came over me this morning, but I was driving my truck down I-20 into Dallas, and as I was going past your exit, my truck just seemed to veer off onto the exit ramp all by itself, so I decided to come on by." Now I was really freaked, but I knew this was the Lord's doing and I had an invitation of love to extend on God's behalf.

I told him, "Larry, I know why your truck veered my direction. God gave me your name in prayer earlier this week, and I've been praying for you every day for the past five days. The Lord has been very clear that He wants a personal relationship with you. He loves you, and He desperately wants you to love Him too."

Larry's eyes welled up with tears as he said, "I know I need to get right with God, but I've got some big messes in my life that I've got to clean up before I can approach Him."

Well aware of the messes he was referring to, I replied, "Larry, you've been trying to clean up those same messes for over twenty years! You're never going to be able to do it on your own. God wants to help you take care of those things. You've got it backward. You think you have to clean yourself up first before you can come to God, but God wants you to come to Him first, then He'll help you straighten out your life."

Our conversation continued, and within an hour Uncle Larry was praying the prayer of salvation on my porch swing. As he did, I sensed the angels cheering and God welcoming His prodigal son home. The next family reunion was also much larger, as Larry brought the sons and grandsons he hadn't been in relationship with since he left his first wife over two decades earlier. Not only did God welcome Larry back home as His beloved son, but He also restored the relationships Larry had missed out on with his own sons.

Today my Uncle Larry is battling skin cancer that has spread to some of his internal organs. While I am concerned about his physical health, I praise God that I don't have to be concerned with his spiritual health. I know I'll get to spend eternity with my dear uncle, and for that I am so grateful.

As you pray specifically for the individuals on your invitation list, don't be surprised if you find yourself with a similar opportunity to be God's representative. You need to be prepared so that when you have such an opportunity, you'll know exactly what you want to say.

KNOWING WHAT TO SAY

When someone asks about Jesus or invites you to share your personal testimony, will you be prepared? Will you know what to say? Will you speak your mind and share your heart about how you are learning to love Jesus without limits? Or will you change the subject or get all tongue-tied?

The past fifteen years of public speaking have taught me the importance of that famous scouting motto—*Be prepared!* While the idea of sharing God's love with others may seem important, many of us stop short for one reason: we don't know what to say. It's not that we don't love God or love the individual; it's a matter of not being prepared with the proper words to express our hearts.

Well, it's time to get prepared! No need to panic. You are not rehearsing an elaborate speech. You are not writing an in-depth research paper. You are not taking a final exam. You won't be expected to preach a sermon about the authenticity of Scripture or present a doctoral dissertation proving that God exists. Your goal is actually very simple: paint a vivid word picture of the difference Christ has made in your own life.

I recommend you start by asking yourself three questions:

1. How would I describe my life today as a result of Jesus' presence?
2. What have been some of the lowest points in my life prior to knowing Him?
3. How has my relationship with Christ made the difference?

Once you've answered these three questions, you are ready to string these pieces of your story together into your own unique bridal story. How? Use this template and fill in the blanks with the answers to the above questions.

Today, I'm living a life that is _____.

But it wasn't always this way. I used to struggle with _____.

Then I recognized God's lavish love for me, and although my life isn't perfect, I am _____.

There's your personal testimony in a nutshell. It is as simple as answering the three questions about what your life is like now, what your life used to be, and how God made the difference.

Why does your testimony need to be this simple? When we get bogged down in academic theories and doctrinal statements, people can always use their own theories and doctrine to debate our knowledge and refute our opinions. But no one can argue with our personal experiences. No one can tell you that Jesus Christ hasn't changed your life in a radical way. No one can tell me that I'm not more fulfilled in my relationship with God than I've ever been with any human relationship. You and I are living these truths. We're staring at the difference every morning when we look in the mirror. We're experiencing bouts of overwhelming joy when there was perhaps little in our lives before. At night when we lay our heads on our pillows, we have a peace that passes all understanding, a peace that isn't present in the lives of those who are unsure about their salvation. We've got something that others should want. We just have to tell them what it is and how they can get it too.

Depending on whom you are talking to, you might want to add another statement that will prompt a personal response, such as "If you are ready for a change in your life, are you willing to give God control?" or "Do you know that God loves you like crazy and wants to have an intimate relationship with you?" Listen to the person's response. Sympathize with his or her struggles. Answer any questions as best you can. Offer to pray with the person and continue to pray for him or her. But start by letting your bridal story create a hunger for an intimate relationship with God.

To give you a clearer picture of what such a testimony looks like, I've gathered a few examples from other women:

- *Pam, age 27:* Today I am a secure and confident woman. But there was a time when I didn't know how to have healthy relationships and my self-esteem was in the gutter. I used to flirt with waiters and scan the room for attractive men that I pretended not to notice. I looked at male drivers in the car next to me at stoplights just to see if they were paying attention to me. I used to dress immodestly to get affirmation and attention from men. But then God began revealing to me through several Bible studies that I am the bride of Christ and that I don't have to stoop so low to get my emotional needs met. He can fill me up with His love. In fact, He fills me up to the point that I'm overflowing and have plenty of love to give to others. It feels great not to be so emotionally hungry anymore. I feel full. I feel loved. I feel special.

- *Terah, age 44:* I now have a wonderful relationship with both my earthly father and my heavenly Father, but it wasn't always this way. My dad's physical and emotional abuse left me scarred and bitter toward him and toward the God who allowed all of that to happen to me. But then I realized that God was as heartbroken over the abuse as I was and that He was drawing me into a healing relationship with Him. He also showed me that it's hurting people who hurt people and that if I could forgive my dad and show him the love of God, I could help ease his pain as well as my own. Things aren't perfect between us, but we're growing closer than I ever thought possible, and I feel more peace than ever before knowing that my dad and I are both in right relationship with God.

- *Angela, age 22:* Nothing gives me greater joy than to reach out to other people, whether it is visiting old folks in a nursing home, reading stories in a children's Sunday-school class, or helping build houses during the summer with Habitat for Humanity. But I used to be incredibly selfish—always thinking about me and what I could get from other people. I acted like a spoiled brat, especially with my parents, insisting that they buy me things I didn't really need and rarely expressing any appreciation.

    But then I went to a concert and heard all about how this band was giving their time and money to help feed hungry children in other countries. These kids didn't have anything at all, but they were so grateful for a little bowl of soup. My heart melted and I knew that God was saying, *You'll never find satisfaction living the way you do. Give Me your life and I'll satisfy you and show you how to satisfy others as well.* I asked Jesus into my heart, and He has blessed me so much that I really want to be a blessing to others whenever I can.

When people hear stories like these, they are bound to recognize there is a God. Why? Because they see Him in action.

MORE POWERFUL THAN YOU REALIZE

Perhaps you are feeling inadequate to share your testimony because you don't have a dramatic conversion experience. Many people have come to Christ without ever having sinful habits or enslaving addictions. It's okay to simply say, "I thank God that He made His presence known to me before I made a total mess of my life."

I had to laugh out loud one day as a young teenager at our house stated matter-of-factly, "I've been a Christian as long as I can remember, but if I didn't have Jesus in my life, I know I'd be a promiscuous wino." I asked her what gave her that impression. She said she's already experienced temptation to be with boys and that when she takes communion, she loves the taste of wine so much that she wants to drink a lot more. She said, "I know that lots of teenage girls fall into these traps and that it's God who has given me the strength not to sleep around or get drunk." While some adults would be shocked by this young woman's words, I applauded her courage to admit her weaknesses and her knowledge that it's only by the grace of God that she hasn't given in to them. That's a powerful testimony.

Margaret Jean Jones, the bedfast woman you read about in chapter 8, never had a radical conversion experience either, yet her love for her Savior is a beautiful testimony to the trust and confidence we can possess as the bride of Christ. In her book *The World in My Mirror*, Margaret writes:

> I never doubted that God was in control. I may have been only an
> eighteen-year-old girl, but I possessed an undying faith. The seeds
> of that faith had been sown many years earlier. I cannot recall ever
> doubting that there was a God. I had grown up in the Baileyton

United Methodist Church. I became a member of that church at the age of twelve and actively participated in its youth organization until I became confined to bed. There had been no dramatic conversion such as Paul experienced on the Damascus Road. Instead, there had been a quietly developing faith, a steady but almost imperceptible assurance of strength that definitely came from outside myself....

I believed completely in the Bible in those early days...and I still believe in it that way. Long years of lying immobile in my hospital bed at home have not diminished my faith in the God of the impossible.[2]

Indeed, some of the most powerful testimonies I know come from believers who have experienced some earth-shattering event long after their conversion to Christ, yet their faith in Him is not shaken. Recently our pastor and his wife, Bob and Stacie Smith, lost their ten-week-old baby boy, Cade, to sudden infant death syndrome (SIDS). With the shock and horror still incredibly fresh in their minds, only minutes after returning home from the emergency room empty-handed, Stacie looked at me while shaking her head from side to side and said, "I do not question God's goodness. He is still sovereign, of that I have no doubt."

Bob also said, "I don't understand it, but I don't want a God I can fully understand. His ways are higher than my ways, and that is okay." This couple demonstrated such rock-solid faith in God even in the midst of indescribable pain and suffering. That's the kind of testimony that cannot be disputed. Who can say there isn't a God in heaven when His strength and peace are so undeniably evident in believers' lives?

Incidentally, if you share your testimony and the person attempts to deny God's sovereignty or disputes our need to submit to His lordship, don't get defensive. If someone doesn't want to believe that Jesus is the Son of God and the only way to heaven, it's not your responsibility to convince that person. After all, people who can be talked into having faith can also be talked out of having faith. People need a glimpse of who God really is for themselves, and that is the Holy Spirit's job. You can, however, help others open their minds to what the Holy Spirit wants to reveal to them by posing the simple question, "What if you are wrong?" Encourage them to explore the eyeopening answers to that question, either with you or on their own. If you are wrong, what will it matter? However, if they are wrong, it will matter a great deal.

A HAPPY ENDING

While we all enjoy different types of stories—comedies, mysteries, romances, dramas, and thrillers—we all crave the same thing. We all want the story to have a happy ending. Perhaps not the cheesy "and they all lived happily ever after" or pie-in-the-sky type of ending, but a conclusion that leaves us with a sense of peace with where the characters end up when the story is over.

One of these days, our stories on earth as we know it will come to a dramatic conclusion. The day of the wedding supper of the Lamb will arrive. Can you imagine a happier, more peaceful ending than to be present at that wedding as a part of the collective bride of Christ, especially when you consider the alternative? Can you imagine the joy you'll experience as you look around and recognize faces in the crowd that are only there because you shared your bridal story and inspired them to embrace their role as the bride of Christ?

All of us should want to go to heaven, but none of us should want to go there alone. Create your list so you'll know to whom you want to toss the bouquet. Prepare your testimony. Share what a difference God's love has made in your life with your friends and family. Apply for a passport, lay it on the altar, and be willing to go wherever God sends you. As you tell of God's lavish love for humanity, continue to eagerly await the day when our heavenly Bridegroom descends to escort us down the aisle into the eternal paradise He's prepared for us.

A Holy Impartation

When Greg and I had been married almost one year, we discovered that I was pregnant. Although this was not part of our plan, we received it as God's and became ecstatic over the little miracle growing inside my body. We shared the news with our friends and family, decorated the nursery, and daydreamed about what parenthood would be like. Two months later, I miscarried.

The idea of having a baby had become such a part of our hopes and dreams that we decided to try to get pregnant again, as soon as possible. It took six months, which may not sound like a long time, but to us it felt like an eternity. I'm sure I drove everyone crazy during that time. Each month I would exclaim, "Oh, I *know* this is it! I *feel* pregnant! I'm tired! I'm nauseous! I'm late with my period!"

But month after month the pregnancy turned out to be all in my head. My hopes crashed down around me with each negative test result. Those were some of the most disappointing and frustrating months of my life. However, through the years I have often gazed upon our incredible daughter, Erin, realizing that if I hadn't miscarried or if I had gotten pregnant any of those prior months, we would have had a different child. I praise God that He united just the right sperm and just the right egg to create such a wonderful human being as Erin Elizabeth Ethridge.

Now, over fifteen years later, I can laugh about how I was able to convince myself month after month that I was pregnant when, in fact, I was not. Some of us do something similar with ministry. We so want to be used by God and have a ministry of our own that we convince ourselves He has called us to do something before the timing is actually right. And what do we usually get when we jump ahead of God? The same thing that Abram and Sarai got.

AN ISHMAEL MINISTRY VERSUS AN ISAAC MINISTRY

God made a covenant with Abram and promised that He would make him the father of many nations. The Lord declared, "Look up into the heavens and count the stars if you can. Your descendants will be like that—too many to count!" (Genesis 15:5). In the Jewish tradition, this was the ultimate blessing one could hope for. But with a barren wife, how could it come to pass?

According to Genesis 16, Sarai did not have the patience or the faith to wait on God, so she took matters into her own hands. Because she had not been able to conceive a child, she instructed Abram to sleep with her servant, Hagar, so they could build a family through her. At eighty-six years old, Abram became the father of Ishmael, who, according to the angel of the Lord, would grow up to become "a wild donkey of a man; his hand will be against everyone and everyone's hand against him, and he will live in hostility toward all his brothers" (Genesis 16:12, NIV).

Doesn't exactly sound like the blessing God promised, does it? That is because Ishmael was born out of the couple's attempt to fulfill God's plan in their own way, when only God can fulfill God's plan.

Fourteen years later, God changed Abram and Sarai's names to Abraham and Sarah, saying that Sarah would indeed still bear a child, even at such an old age (see Genesis 17). Sarah laughed at the notion, and Abraham had the nerve to ask God to alter His divine plan so that it matched their own. "If only Ishmael might live under your blessing," Abraham bargained. God promised that Ishmael would also be blessed, but that His covenant would be established through Isaac, not Ishmael. Genesis 21 tells us that God fulfilled His promise one year later, and Sarah gave birth to Isaac when Abraham was one hundred years old and Sarah was ninety. Talk about late bloomers!

While we might be tempted to criticize the couple for not believing a miracle could emerge from Sarah's womb, then coming up with an alternate plan and expecting God to bless it, don't we do the same? Rather than patiently and expectantly asking God, "What dreams do You want to bring to life through me?" we often ask, "Lord, will You bless the dreams I have for my life?" Our self-sufficiency results in many Ishmael ministries. These ministries ultimately bear human-sized fruit rather than an abundant, God-sized harvest.

In contrast, an Isaac ministry is born of God and is laced with submission, humility, service, and a passion for allowing God to bring His dreams to life, whenever and however He purposes. Isaac ministries bear much fruit and bring great glory to God.

In the words of my friend David Ravenhill (who introduced me to this concept of an Ishmael ministry versus an Isaac ministry many years ago), our dreams are either *self-appointed* or *God-anointed*. We either impatiently will our own dreams for ministry into existence, or we ask the Holy Spirit to impart that which God wants to bring to life through us. John 3:6 explains this biblical principle best: "Flesh gives birth to flesh, but the Spirit gives birth to spirit" (NIV).

Anyone can give birth to an Ishmael ministry. It's easy for flesh to give birth to flesh. However, for an Isaac ministry to be conceived, our spirits must receive a holy impartation from the Spirit of God. If we want to be part of a life-changing ministry, we must intimately connect with the life changer Himself, Jesus Christ.

INTIMATELY CONNECTING WITH CHRIST

Only Adam and Eve experienced intimacy with God to the extent that God intended, walking and talking with Him in the beautiful garden He created for their enjoyment. But because of their disobedience and the resulting fall of humankind, no one since the Garden of Eden has enjoyed such fellowship. We are incomplete, imperfect, and impatiently craving that which our souls simply cannot find apart from an intimate relationship with our loving God.

As the bride of Christ, we eagerly await His return so that our relationship may be perfected once again. We clamor to experience the fullness of God—to hold His hand...sit in His lap...gaze into His loving eyes...feel His warm embrace envelop us...hear His laughter and sense His good pleasure in us. While we will only experience such intimacies and ecstasies with God on the *other side* of heaven, we can still experience great joy in our relationship with Him on *this side* of heaven.

Relating to God so intimately is not a new or strictly charismatic phenomenon. Actually, Judaism is full of wedding and consummation imagery. Each Friday night, *Shabbat* (the Sabbath) is welcomed in as a beautiful bride. The relationship between God and the Jewish people has long been described as that of lovers consummating their pledge to each other.[1] They pursue what was intended from the beginning. They attempt to perfect their love relationship with the Lord. They express their commitment to the utmost degree. They are His people, and He is their God, and they bask wholeheartedly in one another's attentions and affections.

If you are like me, you crave this kind of relationship with your heavenly Bridegroom as well. But we must remember the principle mentioned earlier—*all love affairs are carried on in private*. To experience such depth, we must get alone with God, tune out all distractions, and focus on hearing His voice. This can be a challenge in our fast-paced, hurry-up, gotta-run world. Most of us feel we don't have time to look up, let alone sit still. However, it is true that: "Power flows out of stillness, strength out of solitude. Decisions that change the course of lives come out of these quiet times."[2]

I've learned through trial and error that the more time I spend alone with God, the more effectively I can serve Him. For years I walked and talked alone with God on an almost-every-day basis. I often heard His voice and had a good sense of what He desired of me. Then when we put an addition on our house, we included a workout room complete with a treadmill, television, VCR, and CD player. I began combining my morning exercise with watching a teaching video or listening to a worship CD. However, I soon noticed that writing was becoming a dreaded chore. I'd sit down to write, but energy and inspiration eluded me. One day I asked, "God, where are You? Why aren't You talking to me like You used to?"

I sensed Him responding, *I'm where I've always been—waiting for you to join Me on our daily walks. Why aren't you talking with Me like you used to?* I realized that my video tapes and compact discs had replaced the voice of the Lord in my life, and my two-minute prayers in the shower or while running errands weren't cutting it like my sixty-minute walks used to. Even though I have a workout room to exercise in, I still need regular walks and talks with my Lover. I can't let other things—even really good things—distract me from focusing on Jesus and engaging in the two-way conversation that is vital to keeping my love for Him strong.

Why is an intimate connection with the Lord so important? Because during such times, He imparts in us a passion for the work He wants us to perform on His behalf.

However, perhaps the idea of receiving a holy impartation scares you somewhat, because you suspect some hard labor (and even pain) will be required of you. We'll talk more about this in the next chapter, but for now consider this: *Our love for God should inspire us to want to labor for Him.*

Laboring for the One We Love

Imagine a new bride and how she longs to express her love for her husband. She doesn't just want to sit around and soak up his presence, never doing anything else. She eagerly desires to wait on him and do things for him. She prepares his favorite meal. Launders his clothes. Rubs his back. Takes care of their home where they make wonderful memories together. She doesn't just *love* him, she *labors* for him out of her love.

Such works are a vital part of how a wife expresses her affections. Works are also a vital part of how the bride of Christ expresses her love for her Bridegroom. We can claim to love God, but like my mama used to say, "The proof is in the pudding!" In other words, if we love God we will labor for Him.

The second chapter of James clearly makes this point:

- "Dear brothers and sisters, what's the use of saying you have faith if you don't prove it by your actions? That kind of faith can't save anyone" (verse 14).
- "So you see, it isn't enough just to have faith. Faith that doesn't show itself by good deeds is no faith at all—it is dead and useless" (verse 17).
- "[Abraham's] faith was made complete by what he did—by his actions. And so it happened just as the Scriptures say: 'Abraham believed God, so God declared him to be righteous.' He was even called 'the friend of God.' So you see, we are made right with God by what we do, not by faith alone" (verses 22–24).
- "Just as the body is dead without a spirit, so also faith is dead without good deeds" (verse 26).

James didn't leave any room for misunderstanding on this topic. Labor automatically flows out of our love. If we refuse to labor for God, we may need to question the depth of our love for Him.

We often assume that because God knows our hearts, He also knows that we love Him, even if we don't do anything to show it. However, John Bevere makes a powerful argument against this attitude in his book *A Heart Ablaze.* He observes that in each of the letters written to the seven churches in the book of Revelation, the first words out of the Lord's mouth weren't "I know your hearts," but rather "I know your works."[3] While I believe wholeheartedly that our motives and intentions count with God, I also believe they are measured by the fruit we produce.

It's the same as in marriage. It's not enough for a husband to say, "You know I love you. I shouldn't have to do anything to prove it. You know my heart." A wife wants an active, verbal, or tangible demonstration of her husband's love. The Lord desires the same from us. He made us to worship and to serve Him, which is why we find our fulfillment in both loving Him and laboring for Him.

THE FRUIT OF INTIMACY

Of course, you may be unsure as to how to demonstrate your love or what you could do that matters to God. Perhaps the thought is overwhelming or intimidating. If so, I have good news for you. We do not take the lead in this.

As I watch our kids grow, I am acutely aware that Greg and I had very little to do with their creation. We simply loved each other. We did what came naturally to us during intimate private moments together. We didn't select the genes that gave our children their striking combination of light blonde hair, dark brown eyes, and cute little freckles. God did. He fashioned their forms and breathed life into them. Similarly, God is the One who selects the genetic code of the works He has ordained for us. Only God can impart His dreams into our spirits and fashion them into clear visions. Through intimate time with Him, we can discover what He wants to do *in us* and *through us*. In His perfect timing, we will know when those dreams are ready to come to life.

MY OWN IMPARTATIONS

Even though I've tried to serve God since the late eighties, I will never forget the day that my first "Isaac" ministry was conceived. I had no idea what was happening in the spirit realm. On June 19, 1999, I sensed God saying to me, "I'm placing something within you, Shannon. I'm going to make it grow, and it will be born in nine months." I had never heard of such a concept— God birthing something through someone— so I kept this experience to myself, frequently wondering what was about to happen in me and through me.

Over the next several months, my burden grew tremendously for women who struggle with guilt and shame over their sexual pasts. I longed to give them the guidance I wish I had received earlier in my life. After serving as an advisor to college-age women on the Teen Mania Ministries campus, I offered to lead a growth group on the topic of sexual restoration and emotional integrity in January of 2000. My proposal was approved in February. My first class was scheduled for March 19, 2000—exactly nine months from the date of that holy impartation.

As I prepared to teach this class, I sensed God telling me to write out every word of my lectures rather than speak off the top of my head. *But God, I can manage with a few notes written on index cards!* I argued. However, He clearly directed me to write out every word. Assuming it was so I could give complete lecture notes to any student who missed a certain class, I did it His way.

To my surprise, many young women began asking for copies of my lectures so that they could pass them on to friends. Several expressed an interest in starting their own Women at the Well groups in their home churches or at the colleges they planned to attend. Some aspiring missionaries wanted to use my notes to minister to women in other countries. However, I grew weary of standing at the copy machine hour after hour. I began begging God, *Please show me how I can keep up with You.*"

That was when my dear friend and mentor Jerry Speight recommended that I turn my lectures into a published book. Ironically, Jerry was Gary and Marjorie Jarstfer's neighbor who called me the day of the car wreck. Although I didn't know him at the time of the accident, God reunited us through a random telephone call twelve years later. Following Jerry's advice, I submitted the manuscript to a literary agent, and through a series of divinely ordered events, the lecture notes indeed became my first book, *Words of Wisdom for Women at the Well.*

> *Jesus hasn't led us to [this place] just to make our dreams come true. Our dreams, like the disciples', are always too small. We are here to fulfill God's dream—that we will bring Him glory through a remarkably abundant life. That's how we find our greatest personal fulfillment, now and for eternity.*
>
> —BRUCE WILKINSON,
> *Secrets of the Vine*

Over seven years later, I am still teaching the Women at the Well class to hundreds of young women who want to discover the freedom of living with sexual integrity. This teaching role is one of my greatest passions.

While I can pinpoint the exact moment when I sensed God's holy impartation, I think most Christians gradually discern the work that God has given them to do. What about you? Do you long to bring God's dreams to life but want to be sure you birth an Isaac ministry rather than an Ishmael ministry? Then spend intimate time alone with Him, and ask Him to reveal His dreams to you. You might also spend some time prayerfully determining where your God-given passion lies.

WHAT AM I PASSIONATE ABOUT?

Ask yourself, "What issues tug at my heartstrings? Cause my spirit to ache? Make my heart hurt to the point that I want to do something about it?" Sometimes God uses pain (either personal pain or pain we feel for others) to get our attention and draw us in a particular direction. Other times He uses our joy and excitement. What makes your heart skip a beat and causes adrenaline to course through your veins? Can you remember a time when you were overwhelmed with joy? What gave you such satisfaction and fulfillment?

Here are ten questions to help you search your heart and mind:

1. Is there a particular age group that I feel drawn to? Babies? Children? Teens? Adults? The elderly?
2. Is there a particular group with special needs I feel a passion for? Handicapped children? Inner-city youth? The homeless? Hispanic immigrants? Oppressed women?
3. Is there a particular issue affecting my local school or community that ruffles my feathers or makes my blood boil?
4. What area of ministry at my church appeals to me most? Where do I see myself fitting in?
5. Are there political or global concerns that create a hunger within me to learn more and get involved?
6. If I had to identify the most influential person or factor in my life, who or what would it be? How might I become or pass on such an asset to another?

7. If I had to identify the most traumatic and burdensome issues in my life, what would they be? How can I help others prevent or overcome those same issues?

8. Based on my personality and preferences, what kind of difference do I want to make in this world before I die?

9. What can I see myself wanting to do every day of my life, whether I get paid for it or not?

10. What activities cause me to lose track of time? What gives me a sense of satisfaction upon completion?

Once you identify your true passions, you'll have some valuable clues as to what dreams God had in mind when He created you the way He did. Fervently pray for these passions. Remain sensitive to the Holy Spirit's leading as to how, when, and where God would have you give birth to His dreams.

RECEIVING GOD'S B.B.D.

Regardless of what dreams you have for your own life, God has a B.B.D. (a bigger, better deal) for you than what you have in mind. Just ask Crystal.

Crystal was an eighteen-year-old California girl who had everything. As a beautiful, blue-eyed blonde, she had more than her fair share of male admirers and female followers. She and her friends were into the party scene and all of its entanglements (sex, drugs, booze, cigarettes, and so on). All she wanted out of life was to get married, have kids, and continue to live the fun-in-the-sun California lifestyle.

But God threw a proverbial wrench in Crystal's plans when she attended the San Bernardino *Acquire the Fire* youth convention in the spring of 1999. There she sensed God beginning to impart a new dream in her heart—to leave her sinful lifestyle and go to Texas to participate in Teen Mania's Honor Academy internship program.

Only two challenges stood in her way—finances for the one-year program and faith that God could help her abide by Teen Mania's no-dating rule. Crystal couldn't imagine going without a boyfriend for twelve months straight. Being someone's girlfriend had always given her a sense of identity. She expected she would have to guard her heart like crazy and that she'd surely get involved with some guy the minute she graduated.

DISCERNING WHICH DREAMS GOD WANTS YOU TO BRING TO LIFE

Are you unsure of what kind of ministry God had in mind when He created you? Decipher your calling by discovering your unique personality traits and exploring your spiritual gifts. You may find the following tools helpful:

- *Discovering Your Spiritual Gifts: A Personal Inventory Method,* Kenneth Kinghorn, Zondervan. (A shorter version by VanDruff and Nelson, which is actually built upon Kinghorn's inventory, can also be downloaded for free at: www.acts17-11.com/giftsinv.rtf.)
- *Spiritual Gifts and Church Growth: Modified Houts Questionnaire,* Charles E. Fuller Institute of Evangelism and Church Growth, P.O. Box 989, Pasadena, CA 91102 (626) 584-5350. www.fullerseminarybook store.com.

But that never happened. Instead of having her head turned toward guys, Crystal's heart turned toward God throughout that year. She yearned to give her entire life to Him rather than just the twelve months she had promised. Once her commitment to Teen Mania was complete, she had the option of returning to California, but her dreams had somehow changed. She became a nanny for a family in full-time ministry so she could further explore the idea of doing something similar. While

- *Uniquely You: Combining 16 Spiritual Gifts with 4 DISC Personality Types,* Mels Carbonell, Ph.D., P.O. Box 490, Blue Ridge, GA 30513 (800) 501-0490. www.uniquelyyou.net.
- *Myers-Briggs Personality Test.* Go to www.capt.org/take-mbti-assessment/mbti.htm to take the official comprehensive test online for a fee, or take a similar but less comprehensive test for free at www.similarminds.com/jung.html or www.humanmetrics.com/cgi-win/JTypes2.asp.
- *The Personalities: Personality Testing Instrument,* based on the teachings of Florence Littauer and Marita Littauer, CLASS Services, 3311 Candelaria NE, Suite I, Albuquerque, NM 87107 (800) 433-6633. www.thepersonalities.com.
- *StrengthsQuest: Discover and Develop Your Strengths in Academics, Career and Beyond,* Donald O. Clifton, Ph.D., and Edward "Chip" Anderson, Ph.D., The Gallup Organization, Washington, D.C. www.strengthsquest.com.
- *Servants By Design Inventory.* For more information, go to www.youruniquedesign.com.

traveling throughout Turkey and Afghanistan, Crystal fell in love—not with a man, but with Muslim women. She could almost supernaturally see right through their burkas into their broken hearts. Although these Muslim women dressed far more modestly than typical California girls, Crystal recognized that these women were also looking for love, often settling for sex, and had no knowledge of the God who longed to be the Lover of their souls.

Upon her return to the United States, Crystal finished her bachelor's degree in anthropology with a minor in psychology. For the past six years, she has been a member of a church that sends people into Muslim countries to focus on church planting, evangelism, and campus ministry. Now, rather than spending her time on California beaches improving her tan, Crystal hangs out on college campuses, connecting with women who are hungry to hear about a God who loves them.

She says:

> I would never have caught the vision for reaching out to Muslim women had I just stayed in my own little world. If God had said to me eight years ago, "Move to Turkey and show my love to Muslim women," I would have been too scared to go. It's a good thing He rarely imparts things to us overnight. He gives small revelations and asks for baby steps of obedience. The confidence to pursue these visions is built into our lives over time…day by day, brick by brick.
>
> My emotional wholeness and call to go overseas has been a slow and steady process over the past eight years, and I honestly never thought I'd feel so completely fulfilled. I never believed that my heart could be so healthy, but it is, and it feels so good! The further I venture out of my comfort zone, the deeper I fall in love with Jesus.

When asked about the possibility of getting married while living in a foreign culture, Crystal replied, "What I feel called to is so specific, and there are few men who can lead me in that. I've been open to having a relationship with a man, but I'm not open to abandoning my calling in pursuit of a marriage candidate. I want a husband. I want one badly. But I don't need one. I can be single inside this skin. I'm very satisfied with where the Lord has me. He is all the husband I need."

Willing to go wherever He leads her, Crystal has embraced her role as the bride of Christ, and she is radiant.

Are you willing to do what Crystal did? Are you willing to give God permission to enlarge your dreams if they are too small? Do you trust in His infinitely good and loving nature enough to surrender your own plans and embrace His?

Then refuse to settle for an Ishmael ministry, girlfriend. Don't labor in your own efforts to bring your dreams to life. Rather, expectantly await the holy impartation of an Isaac ministry. Demonstrate your bridal love for Christ by becoming a vessel through which He can bring *His* dreams to life.

When God fulfills His dreams through you, expect an abundant harvest—both in quantity and quality. You will know beyond a shadow of a doubt that you had very little to do with it. You will know full well that God has accomplished the work through you by the power of the Holy Spirit—that He has given you a holy impartation and a blessed opportunity to labor for Him out of your bridal love.

HEARING THE VOICE OF GOD

Twelve Points to Remember[4]

If you know the Lord, you have already heard His voice—it is that inner leading that brought you to Him in the first place. Jesus always checked with His Father (John 8:26–29) and so should we; hearing the voice of the heavenly Father is a basic right of every child of God....

1. Don't make guidance complicated. It's actually hard *not* to hear God if you really want to please and obey Him! If you stay humble, He promises to guide you (Proverbs 16:9).

    Here are three simple steps that have helped us to hear God's voice:

    * *Submit* to His lordship. Ask Him to help you silence your own thoughts, desires, and the opinions of others, which may be filling your mind (2 Corinthians 10:5). Even though you have been given a good mind to use, right now you want to hear the thoughts of the Lord (Proverbs 3:5–6).
    * *Resist* the enemy, in case he is trying to deceive you. Use the authority which Jesus Christ has given you to silence the voice of the enemy (James 4:7; Ephesians 6:10–20).
    * *Expect* an answer. After asking the question that is on your mind, wait for Him to answer. Expect your loving heavenly Father to speak to you. He will (John 10:27; Psalm 69:13; Exodus 33:11).

2. Allow God to speak to you in the *way* He chooses. Don't try to dictate to Him concerning the guidance methods you pre-

fer. He is Lord—you are His servant (1 Samuel 3:9). So listen with a yielded heart; there is a direct link between yieldedness and hearing. He may choose to speak to you:

Through His Word: This could come in your daily reading, or He could guide you to a particular verse (Psalm 119:105). Through an audible voice (Exodus 3:4). Through dreams (Matthew 2) and visions (Isaiah 6:1; Revelation 1:12–17). But probably the most common of all means is through the quiet inner voice (Isaiah 30:21).

3. Confess any unforgiven sin. A clean heart is necessary if you want to hear God (Psalm 66:18).

4. Use the Axehead Principle—a term coined from the story in 2 Kings 6. If you seem to have lost your way, go back to the last time you knew the sharp, cutting edge of God's voice. Then obey. The key question is: *Have you obeyed the last thing God told you to do?*

5. Get your own leading. God will use others to confirm your guidance, but you should also hear from Him directly. It can be dangerous to rely on others to get the word of the Lord for you (1 Kings 13).

6. Don't talk about your guidance until God gives you permission to do so. Sometimes this happens immediately; at other times, there is a delay. The main purpose of waiting is to avoid four pitfalls of guidance: (a) *pride,* because God has spoken something to you; (b) *presumption,* by speaking before you

(continued on next page)

have full understanding; (c) missing God's *timing and method*; (d) bringing *confusion* to others; they, too, need prepared hearts (Luke 9:36; Ecclesiastes 3:7; Mark 5:19).

7. Use the Wise Men Principle. Just as the Three Wise Men individually followed the star and in doing so, were all led to the same Christ, so God will often use two or more spiritually sensitive people to *confirm* what He is telling you (2 Corinthians 13:1).

8. Beware of counterfeits. You've heard of a counterfeit dollar bill. But have you ever heard of a counterfeit paper bag? No. The reason is, only things of value are worth counterfeiting.

Satan has a counterfeit for everything of God that is possible for him to copy (Acts 8:9–11; Exodus 7:22). Counterfeit guidance comes, for example, through Ouija boards, séances, fortune-telling, and astrology (Leviticus 20:6; 19:26; 2 Kings 21:6). The guidance of the Holy Spirit leads you closer to Jesus and into true freedom. Satan's guidance leads you away from God into bondage.

One key test for true guidance: Does your leading follow principles of the Bible? The Holy Spirit never contradicts the Word of God.

9. Opposition from man is sometimes guidance from God (Acts 21:10–14). In our own story, we recognized much later that what seemed like blockage from our denomination was in fact God leading us into a broader scope of ministry. The important thing here, again, is *yieldedness* to the Lord (Daniel

6:6–23; Acts 4:18–21). Rebellion is never of God, but sometimes He asks you to step away from your elders in a way that is not rebellion, but part of His plan. Trust that He will show your heart the difference.

10. Every follower of Jesus has a unique ministry (1 Corinthians 12; 1 Peter 4:10–11; Romans 12; Ephesians 4). The more you seek to hear God's voice in detail, the more effective you will be in your own calling. Guidance is not a game—it is serious business where you learn *what* God wants us to do in ministry and *how* He wants us to do it. The will of God is doing and saying the right thing in the right place, with the right people, at the right time, and in the right sequence, under the right leadership, using the right method, with the right attitude of heart.

11. Practice hearing God's voice and it becomes easier. It's like picking up the phone and recognizing the voice of your best friend…you know his voice because you have heard it so much. Compare young Samuel with the older man Samuel (1 Samuel 3:4–7; 8:7–10; 12:11–18).

12. Relationship is the most important reason for hearing the voice of the Lord. God is not only infinite, but personal. If you don't have communication, you don't have a personal relationship with Him. True guidance…is getting closer to the Guide. We grow to know the Lord better as He speaks to us and, as we listen to Him and obey, we make His heart glad (Exodus 33:11; Matthew 7:24–27).

Giving Birth to God's Dreams

Comedian Bill Cosby used to say that if a man wants to experience the pain of having a baby, he should grab his bottom lip, then stretch it up and all the way over his head! I laughed when I first heard this joke as a teenager, but after my experiences in the labor-and-delivery room, I'm not so sure that Mr. Cosby wasn't on to something!

If you've given birth, you know that before you experience the sweet joy of holding that baby in your arms, you first have to go through a period of discomfort and pain. There's the fear that you will be pregnant forever, as nine months can feel more like nine years. And of course, there is the pain of contractions, labor, and delivery. But then comes the greatest joy most of us have ever experienced—gazing into our child's perfect little face and daydreaming of what he or she may someday become.

The process of giving birth to God's dreams is similar. We go through seasons of preparation, periods of waiting, and times of discomfort and pain before we can experience the joy of giving birth. But that joy is so indescribably wonderful that it makes all the preparing, waiting, and labor well worth it.

Let's take a closer look at the process of giving birth to God's dreams, beginning with the seasons of preparation.

SEASONS OF PREPARATION

In order for us to recognize a holy impartation, we must have a *sensitivity* to the Holy Spirit. We can focus on two areas in particular to prepare ourselves to become as spiritually sensitive as possible—our personal character (what's going on *inside* of us) and our proper positioning (what's going on *around* us).

Sin hinders us from accurately hearing the voice of God in our lives. That's why we must submit to the pain of allowing God to correct and perfect our character. If you are wondering what areas God may want to address in your life, ask yourself, *Where does it hurt?* Through pain, God gets our attention and offers His supernatural healing. Based on the condition of our hearts and our responsiveness to His corrective measures, the healing process can begin with something as simple as receiving a booster shot to remind us of how we should live or as radical as chemotherapy to cure the spiritual cancers eating away at our souls.

Booster shots can come in the form of a thought-provoking passage of Scripture, a convicting sermon or thought, or a warning from a trusted friend. Chemotherapy usually requires more drastic measures, such as the help of a professional counselor or wise mentor. As you've probably gathered from what I've shared in this book, I've experienced both healing processes—spiritual booster shots and character chemotherapy. I've learned to respond more readily to the booster shots so that the rounds of chemotherapy are less necessary. Whatever sins may hinder your spiritual sensitivity, I encourage you to ask God to remedy them.

In addition to being cleansed internally of personal sin, we must also examine what is going on externally in our lives. We must be properly positioned to hear and obey God's voice.

For example, when I first began speaking to youth groups about sexuality, I sought certification for many months from a particular denominational committee. I assumed this would put me in a better position to do what I was most passionate about. At the time, I wasn't aware that the members of this committee were far more liberal in their sex-education methods. Their preference was to literally pass around condoms and birth-control pills so that teenagers could touch them and "get comfortable" with such devices and have "safe sex" if they chose to.

When I presented my plans for a sex-education conference, the committee was miffed that the only things I mentioned about birth-control devices were their incredible failure rates at preventing both pregnancy and sexually transmitted diseases. I didn't want teens to think they could use these methods as a license to have sex outside of marriage. Each member of the committee expressed their belief that I was being naïve and unrealistic to think that teenagers could be expected not to have premarital sex. They felt I should prepare them more effectively. I fought back, believing that their approach to birth-control education was equipping the kids to fail, both sexually and spiritually, and that kids could live up to God's expectations when encouraged to do so.

The several-month battle finally came down to one final meeting where the committee had to make a decision. The good news is that after hours of deliberation, they granted my certification (although obviously very reluctantly). The bad news is that within two weeks the committee announced they were disbanding, rendering useless the certification I had fought so hard to obtain.

At the time, I could not understand why God had me go through all that pain and suffering for what seemed like, in the end, nothing. However, looking back I can now see that God used the committee's resistance to stir my passion for abstinence-based education. He was also positioning me for a much larger audience than one region of one denomination. God's plan for these conferences reached far outside the geographic jurisdiction of that particular committee. My husband and I soon chose to leave that denomination, and God faithfully led us to a new church and new groups of people who would help us reach young people all over the world.

If you have a specific ministry in mind that you know God is calling you to, yet you are experiencing a great deal of resistance from those around you, it may simply be God at work. He may be stirring your passions and testing your commitment. Then again, you may eventually discern that He wants to reposition you into a more supportive environment. Pray and ask for divine guidance, both internally and externally, so that you can maximize your effectiveness in bringing God's dreams to life.

Once you've handed these things over to God, the next part of the process may prove to be a little harder than you think.

PERIODS OF WAITING

Throughout all of my physical and spiritual pregnancies, I've become aware of two things: patience is *not* one of my virtues and stretch marks are inevitable.

For me, the hardest part of giving birth wasn't the labor or delivery but rather the long months of waiting, waiting, and more waiting. I often had dreams that I was allowed to take my baby out of my womb and just hold it and look at it for a while as long as I put it back to finish "baking." Every ounce of my being longed to see, feel, and experience that which would eventually be birthed through me. I didn't want to wait any longer than absolutely necessary. My biological children were very accommodating to my impatient personality. Erin arrived two weeks early, and Matthew came three weeks early. However, spiritual pregnancies don't necessarily follow the same forty-week gestation rule as physical pregnancies. God has His own timetable for bringing His dreams to life, and we must trust that the Great Physician knows exactly when it is time to deliver.

As we are waiting, we will more than likely gain many spiritual stretch marks. Birthing God's dreams may stretch our faith, our finances, and our relationships with family and friends. Remember that God doesn't call us to do things that we can accomplish in our own strength. He only calls us to God-sized tasks, so that when the dream becomes a reality, we know God did the work, and God gets the credit. When ordinary people attempt God-sized tasks, it stretches them tremendously. But this stretching doesn't have to cause us to snap. It can be an extraordinarily strengthening exercise, if we submit to all that God asks of us in the process.

> *Perseverance isn't a lot of fun. Yet it is perseverance that allows God to take our muddled messes and turn them into miracles. He delights in transforming the black-carbon pressures of our life into diamonds of radiant beauty. But doing all that requires a process. A process that takes time. A process that is sometimes painful.*
>
> —JOANNA WEAVER,
> *Having a Mary Heart in a Martha World*

You see, spiritual pregnancies are filled with many moments of waiting, but it is not a passive waiting at all. How can we actively wait? Think of a waitress in a restaurant. She watches as her patrons eat, frequently checking in to see if there is anything else she can do to fulfill their expectations. She is attentive to their needs throughout their dining experience, but doesn't rush them. Or think of a weary traveler waiting for his taxicab so he can return home to his family. He waits on the sidewalk, keeping his eyes peeled for the cab, his suitcase nearby. Think of a young woman waiting for her love to ask for her hand in marriage. She wants him to initiate the engagement, and she diligently communicates her affirming feelings toward him, letting him know that she will not reject his proposal.

Waiting may simply mean returning to the last thing you felt prompted by God to do, then asking yourself, *Have I been obedient?* As a parent, I try not to overwhelm my children by asking them to do something until they have finished the last thing I've asked them to do. God works in similar ways. He guides us step by step, refusing to overwhelm us with the big picture until we can handle it. He doesn't call us to run spiritual marathons until we've been obedient to the little things and mastered basic training.

When was the last time you were certain that God spoke to you? Go back to that place and ensure you have obeyed that instruction. Only then will God continue to give you further direction. That is why it is so important to keep a spiritual journal and record the things you strongly sense the Lord giving you, whether it's instructions, a Scripture verse, an analogy, a dream, or a vision. Obeying each revelation will give you the strength and power to boldly and confidently move forward into your destiny.

Then someday, the season of waiting will be over, and a new kind of pain will take its place.

TIMES OF DISCOMFORT AND PAIN

Just as there is an exact moment when the physical labor process begins, the spiritual labor process is often defined by an exact moment—a moment of decision. Will we give up because of the pain? Or will we push through it and experience the breakthrough we've prayed to receive?

For me, this moment of decision has often come in the middle of the night. For example, as I prepared to write out my first set of lecture notes (which, as mentioned earlier, would evolve into my first book), I was so distracted during the day that I kept putting it off. I was under the impression that I'd write whenever I got around to it. But any writer will tell you that you don't *find* time to write. You *make* time.

So God began waking me up in the middle of the night with a sense of urgency that I must get up and begin working on those lectures. I desperately preferred the sleep over the work, but just as a woman cannot sleep through her labor at the time of delivery, I couldn't return to my slumber. After wrestling with the idea of sleep versus work for an hour or two, I would eventually get up, go to my study, and get on my face in prayer. Many times I begged God through tears, "Please let me go back to sleep! I don't have anything to write!" But God would gently encourage me to sit down at my computer and write the first things I sensed Him saying, as if He were asking me to simply take dictation.

During this period, I posted a sheet of paper above my computer with the following words penned by T. D. Jakes in his book *The Lady, Her Lover, and Her Lord*:

> God...has a plan for you. If you lose your optimism, the enemy has won. Place your hope with the power of God. Place your future in the hands of God.... Don't you know that God had something special in mind when He made you? He had a specific role that only you can play. Refuse to forfeit His plan just because of your pain. Bear it like a woman in labor. Know that the pain will pass, and the promise will be delivered.... This is no time to faint now, dear lady. Grab the sides of the bed and push!...
>
> You cannot stop until you deliver everything that God has implanted within you. I say to you, lady, *Arise!* There is a king within your womb, and he is kicking with life in your spirit. It is the child of destiny, the seed of tomorrow, and the wind of expectation. Do not abort it. Nurture it, squeeze it, feed it, but do not lose it. It is the King. It is the Christ in you. The hope and the glory.[1]

As you labor to bring God's dreams to life, you will more than likely experience many temptations to abort the process. Satan will try anything to get you to give up. So when you feel tired, frustrated, and ready to quit, return to your original vision of what God has asked of you. He will be faithful to do all that He has promised, but you must be faithful to submit to the process.

Fortunately, I learned to submit over and over. I completed my first two books within about eighteen months, and I sensed God was about to do far more with them than I ever imagined.

Just days before I was offered my first book contract from WaterBrook Press, I received the following e-mail devotionals, and I took them as confirmation from the Lord that all of my hard labor was about to pay off and bear much fruit:

August 18, 2001—The water is breaking. Even today you are sensing that something wonderful is imminent.... Something is about to be birthed into the earth.... The water is about to break and then the breakthrough will come that you have longed to see. But more is coming than you have imagined or even prayed to receive. Stand and watch for that is about all you can do. This is my work. The timing is mine.... The water is breaking.[2]

September 8, 2001—Go ahead and give birth. I have been gestating a new thing in you for a season now. It has made you uncomfortable. The discomfort has grown especially strong recently and you have desired to turn back and have had thoughts to abort. But I tell you the victory is in your very hands.... The intense pain right now is necessary. Endure. Crowning is taking place and you can begin to see what I am bringing forth. It is wonderful beyond words. Do not give up. The enemy is standing by licking his lips at the thought that you may decide to abort even now. He never gives up. So now is the critical moment. Seize the moment, take your stand and determine to see this through to the end. The birthing will take place. You will not die even though you feel like you will. I say to you that I will bring you through but you have to push hard right now.... Go ahead and give birth. Amen.[3]

Let these words encourage you as you also prepare to give birth to God's dreams. Know that the joy of a mother's hope fulfilled is so great that all the discomfort you experience up until that moment of birth pales in comparison.

I want to close this book by telling you about another holy impartation and divine encounter I experienced. I share this story, along with the others in this chapter, to encourage you: *The prize of seeing God's dreams come to life through our efforts is well worth all the pain and patience required!*

THE JOY OF GIVING BIRTH

A few months after the initial impartation that I wrote about in the last chapter, I experienced a similar sensation during my quiet time with the Lord one day. This time I recognized it for what it was—and I panicked. My first reaction was, *Oh no, Lord! You've got the wrong girl! I've already given birth to something for You! Don't You remember the Women at the Well class You have me teaching?*

God gently replied, "Shannon, you have two biological children. Just because you had a second one never meant you had to abandon the first one. I'm asking you to birth another dream of Mine. Are you available?"

Immediately Mary's words came to mind when she was approached by an angel and asked to submit to a supernatural impartation of the Holy Spirit: "Behold, I am the handmaiden of the Lord; let it be done to me according to what you have said" (Luke 1:38, AMP). Inspired by Mary's response, I replied, "Yes, Lord, I'm here for You."

During the next several months my compassion for women grew, but not just for college-age women on the Teen Mania campus. I also grew concerned for women of all ages, especially those in parts of the world that don't have access to things that we take for granted in the United States: legal protection from sexual aggressors, reproductive health care, and education about HIV and other sexually-transmitted diseases. One day I was walking on the YWAM campus while praying—no, begging God to help these women. Through many tears I prayed, *Lord, I can't reach them, but You can. They need You. Please give them hope and encouragement. And if You need to use someone, Lord, I'm still available.*

Suddenly, as I continued walking along the trail, I had a mental vision that I was in a labor-and-delivery room—flat on my back, feet in the stirrups, and belly distended. Jesus was standing beside me as my labor coach, holding my hand and saying, "Shannon, you've got to keep pushing! Don't abort the process! Just breathe. Stay focused on Me. Know that I am with you!"

As I continued pushing and praying through a flood of tears, in the vision I saw a full-grown woman emerge from my womb, but I was still very pregnant. Jesus said, "Keep pushing!" and I saw another woman, then another, and another, until millions of women were there in the room with us.

Confused, I looked to my labor coach and asked, "Lord, what does this mean? I don't understand!"

Jesus smiled and said, "Look at their faces, Shannon." That is when I noticed that these women were every shade of brown, black, and white, obviously representing a variety of cultures and continents. Still somewhat confused as to what the vision meant, I went home and read the following e-mail devotional:

June 4, 2001—Oh, what you are about to see! I have been working my plan throughout all the ages. And now in this generation I
will very soon manifest my heart for the world—the whole world.
Do you know how the latitudinal and longitudinal lines are laid
out across and around the entire earth? Have you seen this on your
maps and world globes? But how do you fit in? *You have been gestating for some time now.* There were some truths conceived in your
spirit long before this time in your life. *I caused that conception.*
There has been a time of waiting. At times you have grown weary
and wondered if there was a false conception or perhaps even a
miscarriage. But I say unto you that which was conceived is going
to arrive on time. That time is very near and even now if you can
receive it.... The conception was real in your spirit and what is
about to happen to and with you is in concert with my will worldwide. What you have considered is so much smaller than what I
have in mind. You have dared to reveal my dreams and visions that
I have given you concerning this very thing you will now see. I say
unto you it is real.... Get ready.[4] (italics mine)

Indeed, what I had envisioned was so much smaller than what God
obviously had in mind. A few weeks later, I received the opportunity to
write the Every Woman's Battle book series. Months after I held the first
book in my hands, I received a package in the mail from my publisher
containing another book titled *La Batalla de Cada Mujer* and noticed that
my name was also on the cover. I was holding *Every Woman's Battle* in
Spanish!

The birthing room vision immediately flooded my mind, and I
recalled the beautiful light brown faces, dark eyes, and ebony hair of many
Hispanic women. Over the next few months came a Mandarin translation, followed by Korean, Russian, German, Portuguese, Afrikaans, and

Japanese. Every time I hold a new translation, I marvel that I don't know a single word of any of these foreign languages; yet God, in His divine sovereignty, allows me to be a part of what He is doing in women's lives around the world. As I receive e-mails from countries such as Argentina, Cambodia, Chile, Paraguay, Nigeria, and Singapore, I am astounded. Although I've never visited these places, God has given me the privilege of bringing His dreams to life for women who live there.

So whatever dream God has imparted into your spirit, girlfriend, don't give up. Keep preparing. Keep waiting on God. Keep pushing through the discomfort…and eagerly anticipate a mighty miracle!

FULFILLING THE PROPHECY, RELISHING THE ROLE

When Gary Jarstfer said to me the night before Marjorie's funeral that he was passing her mantle on to my shoulders, I had no idea what he meant. When he challenged me to love Jesus without limits, I hadn't a clue about how to carry that out. But I knew there was something wonderful about both Gary and Marjorie's love relationship with the Lord, and I longed to experience that kind of intimacy with my Creator as well.

As I sought to know Him more, God certainly gave me a glimpse of Himself and His lavish love for me. I received the most extravagant of marriage proposals when God showed me through His Word that Jesus Christ longs for me to be His spiritual bride. He inspired me to forsake all others and taught me the language of love. He showered me with many wonderful wedding gifts and has given me personal demonstrations of His amazing mathematical miracles. He has given me a yearning to toss the bouquet and invite others to an intimate relationship with Him by sharing my bridal story. And He has imparted His desires into my spirit, allowing me the honor and privilege of bringing many of His dreams to life.

As you allow God to do all these things for you as well, I pray you, too, will relish your role as the beloved bride of Christ. Let us never stop learning more and more about how to love Jesus without limits. Let's press on until that day that we get to meet Him (and each other) face to face at the greatest, grandest, most extraordinary wedding the world has ever known!

AFTERWORD
BY GARY JARSTFER

Although August 29, 1984, marks the day of Marjorie's death, God also birthed something special in our hearts that day—a peace that passes all understanding, a deeper trust in His sovereignty, and an unexpected friendship that would glorify God in a magnificent way for many years.

I'll never forget how strongly I felt the presence of the Lord when I received that phone call at a job site in McKinney, Texas. It was my pastor and neighbor saying, "Gary, don't leave. We need to see you. We're on our way." I knew there must be bad news, and I suspected that it had something to do with my wife, Marjorie. When they arrived, my suspicion was confirmed. They explained that a sixteen-year-old girl had hit and killed Marjorie while she was on her morning bike ride. After twenty-eight years of marriage, I would never see my wife again.

They offered to drive me back to Greenville, but I wanted the forty-five minutes alone to think and pray. I knew God was with me, and I could feel Him strengthening me even in the midst of receiving this tragic news.

As I drove, I thought of Marjorie's life and all that she had accomplished. She had accepted the Lord when she was very young, and spent hours reading her Bible and worshiping God through her gift of music, playing the flute, organ, and piano. She had discipled me in many ways, helping me mature into a godly man, husband, and father. We had three grown children who each loved the Lord, and she taught us all by example how to live an extraordinary life of loving others. She was always concerned with other people, and I wanted to react to this situation the way

Marjorie would have if this accident had been the other way around and I had been the one killed.

God clearly reminded me that if I hold any grudges or can't forgive, then He can't forgive me. It says so in Matthew 18. I didn't preplan with anyone what I intended to say to Shannon when I met her for the first time, but I knew that the Lord would lead me in what to say. I wanted whatever words that came out of my mouth to be in accordance with God's will for her. I knew I bore a weight of enormous responsibility. If I said the wrong thing, it could be absolutely devastating to her and perhaps taint the rest of her life. I saw this opportunity to speak into Shannon's life as a chance to bless her, not blame her.

Of course, I didn't have a clue in the world as to what God would wind up doing in and through Shannon's life. I'm absolutely overwhelmed and so grateful for what the Lord has done. I never dreamed she'd become a youth pastor or abstinence educator or an author who would touch so many lives with her writing—it's all so beyond anything I could have ever imagined at the time of the accident. My only hope was that Shannon would carry on Marjorie's legacy of being a godly woman and become as eager to serve Him as Marjorie was. But God has done so much more than that. It's been a tremendous encouragement to me and my family to see Shannon's books reaching vast audiences in multiple countries.

Marjorie was a teacher and an aspiring writer as well, and I believe she would have been so pleased to see the kind of topics Shannon tackles in her speaking and the kind of books she is writing—books that encourage women to live with integrity and to love Jesus without limits. Those are certainly messages that would have resonated with Marjorie's heart.

Since the accident, my family has continued to grow closer to Shannon and Greg, and she is one of our daughters as far as we are concerned. When I moved to North Carolina and married my second wife, Betty Ann (a longtime family friend whose husband was also killed in a car accident just six weeks after Marjorie's death), Shannon was on our list of people to share the good news with as soon as possible. Through letters and e-mails, Betty Ann has been so faithful to keep Shannon in the loop with what's going on in our lives as we've continued to serve with Wycliffe Bible Translators over the past two decades.

We were pleased to get to visit Shannon and Greg while in Texas so we could pray with them and encourage them in their own missionary endeavors. Most recently, we enjoyed several days in North Carolina together with many of Betty Ann's adult children, who consider Shannon one of their own sisters, as well as our grandchildren, who fondly refer to their "Aunt Shannon" as they tell their friends about how Shannon was adopted into our family as a result of the accident. It's been beautiful to see God continue to knit our hearts closer and closer together through the years.

While none of us would have chosen for the accident to take place, we wholeheartedly agree with Romans 8:28, "All things work together for good to them that love God, to them who are the called according to *his* purpose" (KJV). God didn't say only the good things work together for our good. He said *all* things. And He has proven this passage of Scripture to me over and over. I can be at peace with Marjorie's absence on earth and presence in heaven because I know that God is working through her memory to bring glory to Himself—simply because we have chosen to live as Christ lived. We have chosen to bless rather than blame. We have turned tragedy into triumph. We have embraced God's sovereignty and declared that regardless of the pain this life brings, we will forever remain completely His.

A Note from Shannon

Are you looking for a unique idea for a women's retreat? One that will provide an extraordinary experience for women of all ages, from all walks of life? One that will drive home the encouraging principles presented in this book about how we can fully embrace our role as the beloved bride of Christ?

Consider hosting a *Completely His* women's event! Using my four-session DVDs, the special ladies in your church, on your campus, or within your circle of friends will experience the joy of committing their "bridal love" to Jesus Christ, their heavenly Bridegroom.

Because a bride doesn't feel like a bride until she walks down the aisle, this event resembles a wedding ceremony in many ways—a wedding unlike any other you've ever attended, a wedding that will provide a sweet foretaste of the great wedding supper of the Lamb that is yet to come for all of us someday!

My ministry assistants and I have coordinated these events for the past several years for groups as small as ten and as large as four hundred. Here are some personal testimonies about what these events have meant to participants:

> I've frequently heard that I am the bride of Christ, but I never grasped the magnitude of what that meant. But when Shannon gave us an opportunity to attend this event and pledge our bridal love to Christ, it all became powerfully real to me. Now I host these events myself because I want other women to experience the love I've found in my Heavenly Bridegroom.
>
> —Lyn, age 52

Tears of joy flowed freely as I walked down the aisle to unite my candle with Christ's. Even if I get married to a wonderful man someday, no wedding will ever compare to this experience—at least not until I attend the wedding supper of the Lamb when Jesus actually returns for me.

—Tracy, age 20

You have to experience this event to believe how meaningful and life transforming it really is! It's worth every ounce of effort to see women truly feel as if they are *Completely His*!

—Samantha, age 38

For more information, go to www.shannonethridge.com. There you will find plenty of creative ideas, DVDs, and other products, and downloadable forms to assist you in coordinating your own *Completely His* women's event.

NOTES

Chapter 2: Glimpses of a Loving God

1. Loren Cunningham, *Making Jesus Lord* (Seattle: YWAM Publishing, 1988), 95–98. Reprinted from "Right On," by Christian Liberation, Berkeley, California. Used with permission.
2. Haddon W. Robinson, *Biblical Preaching* (Grand Rapids, MI: Baker Academic, 2003), 94–95.
3. Joanna Weaver, *Having a Mary Heart in a Martha World* (Colorado Springs, CO: WaterBrook, 2002), 77.

Chapter 3: An Extraordinary Proposal

1. These points are an adaptation from *The Bible Encyclopedia*, s.v. "Bride of Christ," iLumina Bible Software, Tyndale, 2003. Used with permission.
2. Kenneth L. Barker and John R. Kohlenberger III, *The Expositor's Bible Commentary*, Abridged Edition: New Testament (Grand Rapids, MI: Zondervan, 1994), 1213.
3. Michael Kaufman, *The Woman in Jewish Law and Tradition* (Northvale, NJ: Jason Aronson, 1975), 145.
4. Lisa Aiken, *To Be a Jewish Woman* (Northvale, NJ: Jason Aronson, 1992), 172, 174.

Chapter 4: The Response He Longs to Receive

1. This story was originally written in my first book, *Words of Wisdom for Women at the Well* (Ontario, Canada: Essence, 2003), 17–22.

Chapter 5: Forsaking All Others

1. Shannon Ethridge, *Every Woman's Battle* (Colorado Springs, CO: WaterBrook), 162–63.
2. Nicole Johnson, *Fresh-Brewed Life* (Nashville, TN: Thomas Nelson, 1999), 45.
3. Joanna Weaver, *Having a Mary Heart in a Martha World* (Colorado Springs, CO: WaterBrook, 2002), 9–10.
4. John Bevere, *A Heart Ablaze* (Nashville, TN: Thomas Nelson, 1999), 106–7.

Chapter 6: Becoming Fluent in the Language of Love

1. William Hendriksen, *New Testament Commentary: Exposition of the Gospel According to Mark* (Grand Rapids, MI: Baker, 1975), 100.
2. Max Lucado, *Cure for the Common Life* (Nashville, TN: W Publishing, 2005), 72–74, 76.

Chapter 7: The Ultimate Wedding Gifts

1. Loren Cunningham, *Making Jesus Lord* (Seattle: YWAM Publishing, 1988), 125–27.
2. Randy Alcorn, *Heaven* (Carol Stream, IL: Tyndale, 2004), 179.

Chapter 8: Mathematical Miracles

1. I heard this joke over twelve years ago and have been using it in my speaking ever since. Several variations of the joke can be found on the Internet.
2. Loren Cunningham, *Making Jesus Lord* (Seattle: YWAM Publishing, 1988), 38.
3. Cunningham, *Making Jesus Lord,* 112–13. Used with permission.
4. Margaret Jean Jones, *The World in My Mirror* (Nashville, TN: Abingdon, 1979), 63, 84.

5. Max Lucado, *It's Not About Me* (Nashville, TN: Integrity, 2004), 137–38.

Chapter 9: Living an Irresistible Life
1. *Daily Walk* (Langhorne, PA: Walk Thru the Bible, 2003), July 8.
2. Loren Cunningham, *Making Jesus Lord* (Seattle: YWAM Publishing, 1988), 77–78. Used with permission.

Chapter 10: Tossing the Bouquet
1. Loren Cunningham, *Making Jesus Lord* (Seattle: YWAM Publishing, 1988), 57. Used with permission.
2. Margaret Jean Jones, *The World in My Mirror* (Nashville, TN: Abingdon, 1979), 26, 29.

Chapter 11: A Holy Impartation
1. Rabbi Ted Falcon and David Blatner, *Judaism for Dummies* (New York: Hungry Minds, 2001), 103.
2. Bill Hybels, *Honest to God?* (Grand Rapids, MI: Zondervan, 1990), 25.
3. John Bevere, *A Heart Ablaze* (Nashville: Thomas Nelson, 1999), 104.
4. Loren Cunningham, *Is That Really You, God?* (Seattle: YWAM Publishing, 1984), 161–63. Used with permission from Chosen Books, a division of Baker Publishing Group.

Chapter 12: Giving Birth to God's Dreams
1. T. D. Jakes, *The Lady, Her Lover, and Her Lord* (New York: Putnam, 1998), 65–66.
2. Ras Robinson, Fullness in Christ Ministries, e-mail message to author, Aug. 18, 2001. www.fullnessonline.org. Used with permission.

3. Robinson, Fullness in Christ Ministries, e-mail message to author, Sept. 8, 2001.
4. Robinson, Fullness in Christ Ministries, e-mail message to author, June 4, 2001.

About the Author

Shannon Ethridge is the best-selling author of *Every Woman's Battle* and co-author of the award-winning *Every Young Woman's Battle,* both of which have remained on the best-seller list since their release, and been reprinted in seven different languages.

She's written ten other books, including *Preparing Your Daughter for Every Woman's Battle* and *Every Woman's Marriage.*

Previously a youth pastor and abstinence educator, Shannon has a master's degree in counseling and human relations from Liberty University, and she speaks regularly on the Teen Mania Ministries campus and in a variety of other church and college settings.

She lives in East Texas with her husband, Greg, and their two children, Erin and Matthew.

Visit her Web site at *www.shannonethridge.com.*

LOVING JESUS
WITHOUT LIMITS SERIES

$\mathcal{A}$n inspiring
new series that reveals how
love without limits changes everything—
from best-selling author Shannon Ethridge.